WHEN THEOLOGY
LISTENS TO THE POOR

Mary, The Maternal Face of God
Liberation Theology
Salvation and Liberation
Liberating Grace
Jesus Christ Liberator

WHEN THEOLOGY LISTENS TO THE POOR

LEONARDO BOFF, O.F.M.

translated by Robert R. Barr

1817

Harper & Row, Publishers, San Francisco

Cambridge, Hagerstown, New York, Philadelphia, Washington
London, Mexico City, São Paulo, Singapore, Sydney

FIRST HARPER & ROW EDITION

Library of Congress Cataloging-in-Publication Data
Boff, Leonardo.
    When theology listens to the poor.

    Translation of: Do lugar do pobre.
    1. Liberation theology.   2. Church work with the
poor—Latin America.   3. Mission of the church.
I. Title.
BT83.57.B61813   1988   230'.2   87-46198
ISBN 0-06-254162-5

88 89 90 91 92 HC 10 9 8 7 6 5 4 3 2 1

To my friend Father Lino Bottin, of the Alto da Serra community, near Petrópolis, the good shepherd of his flock, who never "lorded it over them harshly and brutally," or "pastured themselves and did not pasture my sheep"

(Ezek. 34:4, 8)

Contents

Introduction

A viewpoint is a view of things from a particular point or position. What is the most urgent position from which to view reality today? What is the position from which we shall have the surest view of that reality? In Latin America today the answer is clear: the viewpoint of the poor. In Latin America reality must be regarded from where the poor live—from the place of the poor.

By "place of the poor," I mean the cause of the poor, their sacrificed existence, their struggle, their yearnings for life, labor, dignity, and pleasure. The great Latin American masses are made up of poor. The questions raised by the poor affect us all. Who can remain indifferent to the cry of the oppressed for bread and liberation?

To adopt the place of the poor is our first deed of solidarity with them. This act is accomplished by making an effort to view reality from their perspective. And when we view reality from their perspective, that reality simply must be transformed. Reality is exceedingly unjust for the majority of women and men in Latin America. It impoverishes them and pushes them out into the margins of society. To adopt the place of the poor means to assign priority to the questions the poor raise, and then to honestly face up to these problems.

The first question to be confronted is that of life itself. Then come the means of life, such as employment, health, housing, and education. The grandest struggle of the human being is the battle for a bit of bread to be gained by your own toil, for a little piece of ground you can call your own, a humble roof, a minimum of social participation to be won through education. To adopt the place of the poor is to make a discovery. Here we discover the strength of the poor, their resistance, and the dignity of their struggles. They are the needy among us, to be sure. But they are also the agents of their own life and subsistence, the generators of their own dignity and liberation.

To adopt the viewpoint of the poor is to discover the Gospel anew as the Good News of Jesus Christ, Liberator of the victims of every form of oppression. The essays appearing in this book represent an effort to develop theological thought from a point of departure in the place of the poor. We shall never be as the poor. We shall never participate sufficiently in their passion. At most we can be their allies, and bring up the rear. We can be committed to their cause, but never shall we be part and parcel of their crucified lives. And we are still learning. We must grow a great deal if we hope to reach their stature and deserve their communion. We suffer pangs of conscience about our past, about not having been radical, as the poor must be radical. We are tormented at not having had the courage of our convictions. Now we are convinced that Church renewal, and the revitalization of theology, will depend on our approach to the issue of the poor. Christianity's very credibility is at stake here. Small matter the terms in which the Christian message is couched: its credibility will depend on the ability or inability of historical faith to generate hope and liberation. Our Lord has told us that the poor will be the eschatological judges of our practices (Matt. 25:31–46). How much more, then, will they be the judges of our discourse!

The first essay, "Theology of Liberation: Creative Acceptance of Vatican II From the Viewpoint of the Poor," was originally written in German, in homage to my teacher Karl Rahner, on the occasion of his eightieth birthday. It was intended as a token of gratitude for his inspiration during the years in which I studied at the University of Munich, where Rahner taught. Karl Rahner's unexpected death on March 30, 1984, robbed us of the most intelligent and creative theologian of this century. Now he beholds the divine realities on which he so deeply meditated, the realities he helped us surmise and love.

"Mission of the Church in Latin America: To Be the Good Samaritan" was composed in collaboration with the members of the International Congress on *Dives in Misericordia,* held in September 1983 in Collevalenza, near Todi, in Italy.

"Rights of the Poor: Rights of God" is a reflection presented to the First National Congress of Justice and Peace Committees and the Center for the Defense of Human Rights, held in Petrópolis, Brazil, in January 1982.

"How Ought We To Preach the Cross in a Crucified Society Today?" is an address delivered at the Latin American Stauros Congress held in Itaici, Brazil, in October 1983.

The remaining essays in this book owe their origin to a variety of situations—they are all approached, however, within a framework of the theology of liberation. As the audience was different for each essay, there will be some repetition, and I beg the reader's indulgence.

Surely the least that could be asked of a theologian who claims to adopt the Church's preferential option for the poor is an attempt to exercise the ministry of reflection from the viewpoint of the poor and in the interest of their liberation. The theology of liberation is not a fad. To be poor and exploited has never been a fad. Would that it had been, and had gone the way of all fads! Then there would be no more poverty. Everyone would be sharing a just society, a community of brothers and sisters. But let us be realistic, and take as addressed to ourselves the words of Deuteronomy: "The needy will never be lacking in the land; that is why I command you to open your hand to your poor and needy kinsman in your country" (Deut. 15:11). This book is a modest attempt to echo that call of the Lord.

Leonardo Boff, O.F.M.
Petrópolis, Brazil
January 1984

1. Theology of Liberation: Creative Acceptance of Vatican II From the Viewpoint of the Poor

In the context of the Latin American experience of Church, the Second Vatican Council can be regarded from either of two viewpoints. The Council can be seen as the end of a theological and spiritual journey. Or it can be seen as a point of departure for further progress. Both interpretations imply weighty consequences for the concrete life of the Church.[1]

THE COUNCIL AS POINT OF ARRIVAL

The Second Vatican Council can be regarded as the terminus of a long, toilsome process of *aggiornamento.* The Church has finally succeeded in adapting to the modern culture in what was the upshot of the bourgeois revolution—an upheaval in economic, scientific, technological, and political expressions.[2]

Our modern culture arose in the margins of the Church, almost always without the Church, and, often enough, against the Church. Various Christian movements, however, through equally varied practices of insertion into the spirit of modernity, have embarked upon a new codification of faith in response to the challenges of today. This is the deeper meaning of Christian liberalism, religious socialism, modernism, and the so-called Nouvelle Théologie. There is no need to recall here the drama of the ecclesiastical repression that burst over the heads of the proponents of these movements. But this only delayed the inevitable *aggior-*

namento. It never succeeded in rendering it totally inviable.[3] It was urgent that church leadership fall in step with contemporary historical time, lest the Church become a stronghold for reactionaries of every hue and stripe, a fossil from a bygone world, to the detriment of the credibility of the Gospel.

The Second Vatican Council assumed the task of examining and setting forth the Christian message "by means of the research methods and literary formulation of modern thought" (John XXIII, Opening Discourse of the Second Vatican Council, October 10, 1962). Vatican II thought of itself as a pastoral council then. Its first priority would be mission. Church reorganization and renewal would be in function of the Church's mission *ad extra.*

In function of mission, the Church of Vatican II now welcomes that modern world whose victories it once so strongly questioned. Now the Church is partisan of freedom of conscience and thought, freedom of religion, the autonomy of terrestrial realities (eventually dubbed secularization), and the democratic spirit. Now the Church esteems the human person in his or her sacred subjectivity, historicity, and transforming dynamism. Now the Church proclaims the oneness of human history. The task of the Church is but to interpret that single history in its aspect as the history of salvation. Now the various Christian Churches are discovered as realizations, however incomplete, of the Church of Christ, and this is the theological basis of ecumenism. Now the Church takes up the challenge of the religions of the world in all their significance for salvation history. Now the Church welcomes a dialogue, *ad intra* as *ad extra,* as a path to consensus, in the spirit of a mutual apprenticeship and a mutual enrichment, with respect on all sides for the pluralism of our modern world.

The Church of Vatican II seeks a self-understanding within a modern, secular, pragmatic world that is jealous of its autonomy, that is impregnated by the spirit of emancipation, whose hallmarks are production and a rate of development that makes one's head swim. It is in the world, and not out in the margins of the world, or without the world altogether, that the Church means to be the sacrament of unity among human beings and unity between humanity and God. When the council documents speak of the human being, it is the concrete human being of enlightened culture who is meant, the citizen of an advanced society.[4] During the actual course of the Council, a new ecclesial consciousness developed. The Church became aware of its insertion in the modern world. The Pastoral Constitution *Gaudium et Spes* represents the outcome of this shift in the Church's center of gravity. From a position of ecclesiocentrism, the Church has slowly moved to a "mundocentrism." The opening sentence of this landmark document portrays the Christian's new spirit of solidarity with the women and men of today, especially with the poor and with all who suffer in any way.

The Second Vatican Council projects an atmosphere of optimism, of openness in all directions, of reconciliation with the finest yearnings of modernity, especially with the spirit of work, with science and technology, and with dialogue among cultures. The Church offers its services in the construction of peace and the promotion of a community of peoples. The Church is sensitive to the dramatic misery of the poor. At the same time an attentive analysis will reveal that this new approach on the part of the Church is circumstantial. It is adopted in a framework of the great, modern society of opulence. To be sure, the observation is made that "luxury and misery rub shoulders," and that "numerous reforms are needed at the socio-economic level, along with universal changes in ideas and attitudes" (*Gaudium et Spes,* no. 63).[5] But there is no clear consciousness yet of the causal, structural nexus between luxury and misery, nor any inquiry into the nature of the reforms demanded. Ought these to be applied within the prevailing system (reformism)? Or ought we to have a new kind of society altogether (liberation)?

At all events, with the Second Council of the Vatican the Church has made a worthy effort to define its place and mission in the modern world. This point of arrival was indispensable to any further advancement.

In recent years the official organs of power in the Church have tended to regard the Council simply and solely as a point of arrival. This tendency has received particular emphasis in its juridical expression in the new Code of Canon Law, in effect since November 27, 1983. Here the council texts are subjected to a neoscholastic treatment, and employed as authoritative texts in the spirit of the old dogmatic councils. Their intended pastoral character, and hence their orientation to practice, is forgotten. Thus we see an effort to apply the brakes to certain advances, along with an attempt to create a new doctrinal homogeneity in the Church. This is what seems to be meant by the frequent references of the Magisterium to the "legacy of the Second Vatican Council."[6]

In the face of this tendency toward officialism, it would be well to recall the words of Pope Paul VI in his letter to the Congress of Postconciliar Theology, September 21, 1966: "The task of the Ecumenical Council," writes the Holy Father, "is not brought to its final conclusion with the promulgation of the council documents. The latter, as the history of the councils teaches, represents a *point of departure* rather than the attainment of a goal. It remains for the entire life of the Church to be impregnated and renewed by the vigor and the spirit of the Council. The seeds of life sown by the Council in the field that is the Church must come to full maturity."

The Holy Father is clearly aware of the need for "thinking" the Christian message beyond the point reached by Vatican II—the need to develop a new articulation of the "intelligence of the faith" in the context of the modern world. The Council has charted the course. It remains for us to follow this new route, and not merely to devote ourselves to the labor of an exegesis of what has already been said and written in the conciliar pronouncements.

This exigency has stirred various theological tendencies in the countries of the "center," and these new theologies appeal to the spirit of Vatican Council II as their basis and support. The first of these is the so-called *theology of secularization,*[7] which comes on the scene as a demand for the autonomy to which modernity lays claim. The theology of secularization demands the right of self-determination for organs of political, scientific, economic, and anthropological rationality. The theology of secularization has made a contribution of permanent value: in its presence we can no longer fail to be aware that the objectively theological *(le théologal)*—God's design, grace and salvation, sin, and so on—is not verified only where there is theological consciousness *(le théologique)*, but constitutes a fundamental dimension of all reality and all human practice, which in the concrete either is ordered to the building of the Reign of God or is not. The Church is no longer regarded as the sole mediator of God's grace and historical project. The Church presupposes the objectively theological—the ongoing history of salvation—and becomes the sacramental and reflexively theological sign of this material theological element, as well as the instrument of its more explicit historical implementation.

Next comes the *theology of the political.* Political theology is one of the finest currents of thought to emerge from the intuitions of the Vatican II.[8] It takes up the challenges of the Enlightenment anew, along with those of that broader horizon of our culture, the realm of the political. It seeks to deliver the Christian community from the intimistic and privatizing distortion to which the message of Jesus has been subjected. It seeks to recover the "perilous memory of Jesus," who died a death for all the world to see amidst the paroxysms of a struggle for power. Political theology, as Johannes B. Metz vigorously puts it, is as an "attempt to place the eschatological message of Christianity in a relationship with the modern age as a form of critical practical reason." Here Christianity hopes to do more than improve religious expression. It means to collaborate in the construction of the new human being.

Third, we have the *theology of hope.*[9] Initially of Protestant origin, this new theology was quickly adopted by a good many Roman Catholics as well as faithful of other religious groups. From one point of view, the theology of hope is a kind of theology of the political: it seeks to translate eschatological hope into a principle of historical transformation, into utopias, projects, and revolutions calculated to concretize, on the sociohistorical level of our own age, the good things that have been promised only for the end of time.

Finally, the intentionality of a *theology of revolution*[10] appears to funnel Christian action straight to the heart of the world's wickedness, where the levels of violence are so intense that they provoke a response of revolutionary antiviolence, and the very structure of society is transformed. This theology is not "made in Latin America," as has been claimed. It has emerged from the matrices of the wealthy societies themselves—as simple reflection, it is true, without practical consequences—as "an attempt at filling the historical vacuum felt by Christians" who see that they have no impact on society.[11]

These new theologies constitute serious attempts to go forward with the spirit of Vatican II. And they address the issue of modernity. But the addressees are modern, enlightened, critical men and women, who pose their questions in terms of the relationship between science and faith, the private sector and the public, the present and the future, theism and atheism. The poor, the vanquished, enter into consideration, of course, as we see clearly in the reflections of Johannes B. Metz and Jürgen Moltmann; but they only come into consideration by way of subthemes within the broader issue of modernity.[12] The Council, for these admirable currents of Christian thought, has been more than a mere *terminus ad quem*—except where context, or an issue made up of relevant questions, is concerned.

In saying this I do not mean to belittle the merit of these new theologies. They have taken up current questions with courage and determination. They have thought them through in categories and in a language relevant to modern thought.[13] Their merit is great. But they have one large shortcoming. In confrontation with church practice they become strangled. Rarely has any of them been the occasion of a transition from theology to an alternative practice on the part of the people of God. The concrete effect of these new theologies in terms of the animation of church life, in terms of a gestation of new movements and styles of expression of faith, has remained inchoative. To be sure, responsibility for this fact lies less with the theologies themselves and the intentions of the theologians and their disciples than with the weight of ecclesiastical tradition and the controlling power of the organs of church authority. New thoughts have produced but other new thoughts. There is no significant break with the past, no substantial move in the direction of a new way of being Christian and being Church, no articulation of theory with practices aiming at the transformation of society, and within society practices aiming at the transformation of the Church.

THE COUNCIL AS POINT OF DEPARTURE

The presence of the bishops of Latin America at the Second Vatican Council had no theological impact. One even heard of a "church of silence." But the Latin American episcopates made a rich contribution of another kind. Their impact was in the pastoral area. The Latin American bishops voiced the restlessness of the poor. They made the universal Church aware of the issue of social justice.[14] The National Council of Brazilian Bishops had been established before Vatican II, in 1952. A joint pastoral experiment spanning the entire country was under way, an example of the collegial exercise of episcopal authority. CELAM, the Council of Latin American Bishops, was created in Rio de Janeiro in 1955. Even a pancontinental pastoral experiment was in progress. Prophetic minorities under the leadership of Dom Hélder Câmara in Brazil and Dom Manuel Larraín in Chile had learned to grasp and interpret the principal elements of human reality and the mission of the Church within that reality. (Prophetic minorities, always both in communion with the universal Church and solidly inserted into current historical reality, should not be confused with an elite vanguard deprived of this popular insertion.) These influenced the course of the conciliar sessions and the definition of thematic priorities. Dom Hélder Câmara and Dom Larraín were the individuals mainly responsible for the creation of two unofficial groups that provided a locus of encounter among bishops from all over the world, especially those from the Third World and others especially sensitive to sociohistorical problems: "Le Christ et l'Eglise servante et pauvre" ("Christ and a Poor Servant

Church") and "L'Eglise et l'aide aux pays en voie de développement: conditions d'une action efficace" ("The Church and Aid to Developing Countries: Conditions for Effective Action"). The debates held at the Brazilian bishops' hospice, Domus Mariae, drew the best theologians of the Council—such as Karl Rahner, Edward Schillebeeckx, Yves M.-J. Congar, Jean Daniélou, and so on—and helped create the pastoral spirit of Vatican II.

The Second Vatican Council had an enormous impact on the Latin American Church. The spirit of the Council, together with its corpus of documents, wrought two decisive effects here. First, a church renewal already well on its way now enjoyed official legitimation. Second, now it would be possible to implement a creative acceptance of the Council from a point of departure different from that of the Council's own conception, realization, and development: the point of departure being the viewpoint of the poor.

Both of these effects deserve closer examination. Since the 1960s an economic, political, social, and ideological crisis has held nearly the whole of Latin America in its grip. The prevailing model on our continent is that of dependent capitalism characterized by rapid industrialization and urbanization.[15] Large foreign concerns have installed themselves in various countries here. Instead of importing materials or products from abroad, these corporations, under license and encouraged by hefty fiscal incentives, manufacture their products here in our countries, using our abundant raw materials and our cheap labor.

In the beginning the euphoria of developmentalism reigned, especially during the administration of John F. Kennedy and the 1961–69 Alliance for Progress. Keeping pace with the accelerated productive process, however, the level of consciousness of the laboring class was being raised with respect to the degree of exploitation and marginalization to which they now saw themselves subjected. There was development, indeed, but the price was paid by the people and the benefits went to the traditionally affluent Latin American elite and their foreign partners. The union movement began to grow. So did other popular movements. New demands on the part of the people began to threaten the hegemony of the bourgeois classes and bourgeois state. University students mobilized, intellectuals joined the ranks of the people. A scientific reading of the underdeveloped reality of Latin America from the viewpoint of the underdeveloped themselves showed that the relationship obtaining between the center and the periphery was one not of genuine interdependency, but of dependency pure and simple, which in moments of crisis would blossom into full-fledged oppression and block any needed social transformations. The history of the oppression of the Latin American continent was continuing unabated. A process of liberation had to be set in motion.

The political mobilization of the people enjoyed the participation of a good many Christians, especially in the university pastoral ministry. It became clearer and clearer that our underdevelopment was not primarily a technological question—a matter of not having kept up with technological developments—but a political one. The political strategy in force was geared to maintaining countries under the same type of economic and political regime, with a formal democracy and also with a wealthy elite exercising its hegemony either directly or via a welfare state, thus maintaining control over the people and their organizations.

Within this overall strategy a "peripheral capitalism" appeared, dependent on the capitalism of the "center," the wealthy nations of the northern hemisphere—Europe and the United States. It became clear that it was this center that was responsible for the misery of the people. It was the long arm of peripheral capitalism that was throwing up obstacles to any necessary social or economic transformation, via on-the-scene political and military repression. The bishops of Latin America, as in Brazil, for instance, often assumed a leadership role in the task of the "conscientizing" and collaborating with the people. The first base church communities date from as early as 1955. The Base Education Movement, along with the religious education of the oppressed begun by Paulo Freire, were under way. More and more Christians were becoming militant, all over the continent, and were joining popular organizations or left-leaning political parties, and proposing alternatives to projects supported by representatives of the status quo.

Close upon the heels of this praxis followed a faith reflection. These were the years when so much reflecting was done on Christianity and development, faith and revolution. The people, almost in their totality, were Christian. There was no "death of God" down here. But the "death of the people" was in full swing, at the hands of a death-dealing social system that reduced men and women to the status of subhumans. The key question of the 1960s—and still the great question assailing the Christian conscience in Latin America today—was, What does it mean to be a Christian in a world of the oppressed?

Little by little the only response possible emerged. The only way to be a Christian was to be at the service of liberation. We did not just happen to be underdeveloped countries. We were maintained in underdevelopment by oppression. In our lands *poverty* meant forced impoverishment at the hands of economic and social mechanisms of exploitation.

By now the word *liberation* had become a slogan in the mobilized groups of our society. Liberation was the opposite of oppression; liberation was whatever oppression was not. For us in Latin America the word came out of a precise historical context. It recalled our continent's revolutionary processes—in Mexico in 1911, in Bolivia and Guatemala in 1952, in Cuba in 1959, in the resistance that met the United States invasion of Santo Domingo in 1965, and in the countless guerrilla movements of so many other countries, such as Colombia, Peru, Brazil, Argentina, and Uruguay. Liberation took a step beyond developmentalism. Ultimately, developmentalism unfailingly bolstered the prevailing exclusive, elitist social structure.

A prerequisite for liberation is a break with the conventional attitude and activity of society and Church alike. You must adopt the attitude of the poor and act against their oppression. You are in favor of the poor, and against their impoverishment. Two historical figures embody the ideals of liberation and continue to have an enormous impact on groups committed to qualitative changes in society. They are Argentinean Ernesto ("Che") Guevara, who was killed October 8, 1967, and Colombian Father Camilo Torres, killed February 15, 1966.[16] Each had chosen a revolutionary option. Each was inspired by the cause of the liberation of the forgotten ones of Latin America—the peasants, the proletarians, the poor. Each died fighting for this cause.

As a capitalistic state consolidated its defenses against an organized people, the liberation movement consolidated as well. Political and military oppression now entered a genuinely militarized stage. Now this oppression was organized in more coordinated and consistent fashion, and all political parties, unions, and other groups and movements that called for substantial changes in society were methodically persecuted.

This was the context in which the documents of Vatican II reached Latin America. They were read in a sound box that made the spirit and main themes of the Council come alive with meaning. Vatican II was seen as granting universal endorsement to a regional church that had opened itself up to the world, the poor, and social justice. True, the mentality of the Council fell short of the critical social awareness that had been reached by our committed Christian groups. But the institutional support the Council lent to the efforts of these groups was priceless. The Council gave sanction to a church engaged in the social arena, a church involved in the lot of the abandoned of this world. It was as if the Council lived in Latin American practice first and then was embodied in verbal and written form in Rome. The council documents seemed to confirm, reinforce, make official, the stretch of the road that Latin America had already traversed.

The atmosphere was ideal for courageous theology. At the Tenth Assembly of the Council of Latin American Bishops, held at Mar del Plata, Argentina, in 1966, Dom Hélder Câmara, prophetic herald of the Church of tomorrow, could now proclaim:

A human being free and aware, a human being engaged in a gradual *liberation* from a thousand servitudes: behold our goal. Men and women whose basic freedom will grow, and grow, until they reach such a pitch of freedom that they will be free to deliver themselves from themselves, and so be able to bestow themselves on others.

The quantum leap occurred in July 1968, with Gustavo Gutiérrez's celebrated address in Chimbote, Peru, entitled "Toward a Theology of Liberation."

CREATIVE RECEPTION OF THE COUNCIL FROM A STARTING POINT IN THE PERSPECTIVE OF THE POOR

The theology of liberation originates in Christian practice. Its theologians are priests, religious, and laypersons committed to a qualitative change in a society of destitution.[17] The originality of this new way of doing theology does not reside in the fact that it specifies oppression-and-liberation as the object of its reflection. Any way of doing theology can address this issue, nor indeed has the latter ever been missing from any theological current. This material object does not of itself oblige theology to change methods or structure. It is perfectly possible for a theology to approach the subject of liberation with the same tools with which it approaches the divinity of Jesus, the fatherhood of God, grace, or sin. Indeed, this is precisely the basis of the various "hyphenated" theologies of past decades—theologies of labor, of sexuality, of secularization, of the city, and so on.

No, the uniqueness to which the theology of liberation lays claim is that of being a faith reflection originating and developing within the actual practice of liberation. Let me be very clear: liberation theology is not a reflection on the theoretical subject of liberation. It is a reflection on the concrete practice of liberation engaged in by the poor and by their allies in the field of their struggle. By reason of their very faith commitment, Christians commit themselves to the cause of the poor and their effort to change society. We must have a society marked by more of the characteristics of the Reign of God—justice, popular participation, human dignity, and a communion of brothers and sisters—than we have today. It is within this practice that Christians seek to understand the whole content of Christian faith.

At this point a new way of doing theology arises. Now theology is done from a point of departure in political practice, from the heart of a commitment to solidarity with the oppressed, with the goal of liberation ever in view. The "first word" belongs to practice—practice in the pregnant sense of lucid, conscious action calculated to be the vehicle of a historical project.

The practice of which we speak in a context of the theology of liberation is maintained at several distinct levels.[18] First comes the *pastoral* level. A liberative pastoral approach asks, What pastoral ministry, what ecclesial practice, will help a people of the poor to have their consciousness raised, to become "conscientized," with respect to the sin of oppression of which they are the victims, and to enter into the grace of solidarity and the birth of justice? What sort of religious education, what kind of liturgy, what kind of homiletics, what way of celebrating the sacraments, is genuinely the Christian way from the viewpoint of the oppressed? Does such and such a pastoral approach leave Christians indifferent to the problem of oppression? Or does it encourage them to embark on a practice enlightened by Christian faith and revitalized by the celebration of the sacraments? In other words, which Christian practices produce changes in the direction of justice?

Next there is the level of *the Church and the political.* Here the questions are, What are the political and social practices in which Christians engage? Does Christian militancy merely reinforce a situation that is demonstrably wicked and unjust? Or are Christians being incorporated into movements for social transformation that aim at a society of greater popular participation, a society in which the poor are heard and their needs met? The Church is deeply divided here. There are Christians (laity, bishops, and pastoral ministers) who both in theory and in practice simply reinforce the status quo, who develop no propheticism, and who relate to the poor in a purely assisting, paternalistic way. There are other Christians who form ties with the popular classes, who take up the cause of the poor, and who move outward from the specificity of their faith to a contribution to a new social awareness and new structures of reality.

Finally there is the level of the *political* in the strict sense. Here, Christian practice means any influence brought to bear on the structures of society with a view to their transformation to the benefit of the wretched of the Earth. In Latin America it is the popular classes *in toto,* and not only the Christians of these classes, who have the greatest interest in a qualitative change in society. Any such liberation practices, in the measure in which they actually liberate—to the extent that they actually restore the despoiled to justice and the oppressed to dignity, making the downtrodden the agents of their own history—advance the process of God's project. Such practices, no matter by whom performed, render the marks of the Reign of God things of the present.

The theology of liberation, then, begins with actual liberative practice. Its aim is liberative efficacy. It makes itself responsible for an analysis of social, conflictual reality, of course, and has its starting point in the outlook of the poor. But this analysis is not an end in itself. Its raison d'être is the transformation of the reality thus analyzed. Liberation theology is not satisfied with a more adequate interpretation of social reality and a consequent theological reading of that reality. It is possible, of course, for a theology to achieve this and no more. And indeed this is what other theologies frequently do. But this alone fails to manifest the methodological originality of the theology of liberation. This is mere interpretation—analytical, then theological. No, the decisive moment is that of a transforming activity: a transforming praxis, in a concrete engagement with groups constituted for reflection and action. At the heart of this real commitment, this commitment to reality, a theological reflection, subdivided by theme, is developed.[19] No longer is the theologian a mere professor, just a specialist in religion. Now he or she is also a militant.

Liberation theology, then, is a critical reflection on human praxis—the praxis engaged in by men and women in general and Christians in particular—in light of the practice of Jesus and the exigencies of faith. Jesus' practice obviously reserved a special place for the poor. For Jesus, not just any kind of action was action worth undertaking. This is what placed him at odds with various elements of established authority and finally resulted in his death. The Reign of God begins with the poor, and only then extends its embrace to include all men and women.

What Is "Creative Acceptance" (Receptio)?

Consistently, creatively, this new way of doing theology has assimilated the spirit of the Second Vatican Council. The theology of liberation is an acceptance of the meaning of the Council in a framework of the religious and political interests of the poor. This is the main reason why I have said that Vatican II has been a point of departure for further developments in the Church in Latin American society.

This process of acceptance is known in theology by the technical name of *receptio*. [20] It is most commonly defined as "the process by which an ecclesial body assimilates and appropriates a determination originating without, acknowledging it as a rule for itself in the measure in which it is promulgated and is appropriate for its own life."[21] In this definition true *receptio* is the act of receiving, welcoming as one's own, something that comes either from above (as, for example, the definitions of a council or determinations of a continental or national bishops conference) or simply from without (as would be the case in an Eastern Orthodox acceptance of a Roman Catholic decision, or if Roman Catholics were to execute a *receptio* of some consensus reached by the World Council of Churches).

In early Christian times the accepted concept of Church was expressed in the category of communion. In function of the special relationship obtaining among the various churches, a *receptio* of one another's doctrinal, disciplinary, and liturgical determinations prevailed. This process of *receptio* through communion found a special application in the context of the ecumenical councils.[22] The First Council of Constantinople (381 A.D.) "received" the Council of Nicaea (325 A.D.), the Council of Chalcedon (451 A.D.) "received" the First Council of Constantinople, and so on. In the field of church law, from the earliest decretalists onward, we hear of an "appropriative" and an "executive" *receptio.* [23] In later, ecclesiastical times we see the force of *receptio* in the development of dogma, and finally today in the area of ecumenism, as an effort is made to reestablish an acknowledgment of the ecclesiality of the various Christian churches and a communion among churches separated and deprived of dialogue for centuries.

Normally *receptio* involves a passive process where content is concerned. What has been developed by others is received positively, welcomed. The pope receives the documents of Vatican II elaborated by the bishops. The faithful receive the documents of the Council as promulgated by the Holy Father in solidarity with the conciliar fathers. A process of appropriation takes place. A rule or other determination is received because of its utility in the edification, the upbuilding, of the faith of Christian communities. Of course, the rule or determination does not depend on this reception for its validity. The authority of an ecumenical council conjointly with the pope, for example, is the font of the validity of its own laws. But a determination depends on its acceptance in order to be *efficacious.* A rule or other determination is efficacious when, over and above its formal juridical quality as valid (which per se is insufficient for efficacy), it is also appropriate—when it is responsive to the exigencies of the life of faith and the common good of the faithful.

Receptio in this full sense is not simply synonymous with obedience, in the sense of submission to the will of another out of love of God or of church unity. Acceptance wins ecclesiological status when there is a *vital embodiment* of the content proposed by ecclesiastical authority—when acceptance of the content in question both enjoys a consensus and occasions an increase in the vigor of the Christian life. Nonacceptance on the part of the community of believers does not, in and of itself, mean disobedience. It may merely be a sign that the determination in question either does not pertain to the deposit of faith after all, or that even if it does, it does not foster the common good, perhaps because it is not opportune for the conditions of the time and the religious needs of God's people. A typical case was that of the pontifical constitution *Veterum Sapientiae* of Pope John XXIII, published in 1960. This papal instrument was solemnly proclaimed, was attended by all of the symbols of sacred power—and remained splendidly inefficacious. It had sprung from a pure voluntarism—an act of the will that it *be* good for the faithful. It was not an actual expression of the common needs of the faithful in the prevailing context of genuine pluralism.[24]

On the other hand, the definition of *receptio* is not exhausted simply in a sincere welcome of what is proposed to the community by its pedagogues in the faith. *Receptio* is not only passive. It is active as well. This is the point I wish to emphasize here. Once passively received, a given rule or other determination may undergo a process of elaboration in depth. Other meanings may now be derived from the raw content of the received determination itself as the latter is subjected to an active development of its original sense. Only now is the *receptio* in question vital and alive. The people of God have the right not only to receive the whole truth of faith, but also to elaborate, to develop it within a contemporary codification. In other words, the people of God have the right to place their own emphases, to make their own discernments as to which perspectives of the received content are relevant to the various particular historical situations with which they are confronted.

With regard to the diversity of the situations in which Christians of today's world find themselves, the papal magisterium has acknowledged that "it is difficult both to pronounce a single world and to propose a solution with universal value." But this—said Paul VI—"is not our ambition, nor indeed our mission. It pertains to the Christian communities . . . (and to the) unchangeable words of the Gospel."[25]

In this purview we might think of the theology of liberation as claiming to be an expression of the social thinking of the Church, particularly in Third World situations, and thus claiming the right to an ongoing development in a context of confrontation between historico-social reality and the joint social doctrine of the Gospel message and the accumulated teaching of tradition.

The ultimate justification for creative reception in ecclesiology lies in a sane epistemology of the act of faith. Pastoral practice can only profit from a correct theoretical discourse, in this area as in any other.[26] According to an intelligent epistemology, the meaning of a text (setting forth, for example, a rule or some other determination) emerges not only from the minds of the authors of the text (from the *mens patrum,* in the case of a conciliar text) and the words used by these authors (the literal meaning of the text)—but also from the addressees, who are coauthors of the text, inasmuch as it is they who insert the message of the text into the vital contexts in which they find themselves. The addressees, too, place accents, and perceive the relevancy and pertinence of aspects of the text in question that illuminate or denounce historical situations. The original meaning of the text—the meaning contained in the "letter"—stirs new echoes when that text is heard in determinate circumstances. The spiritual meaning becomes revealed. To read, then, is always to *re*read. Whenever we understand, we interpret; this is how our spirit is structured. The original message does not remain a cistern of stagnant water. It becomes a font of living water, ready to generate new meanings, by prolonging and concretizing the original meaning. The latter functions as a generator of new life through the new significations it awakens.

How Latin America Came to a Creative Reception of Vatican II From the Viewpoint of the Poor

In light of the preceding considerations you now understand more clearly that the Second Vatican Council is still in process. It has not closed off its historical impact against all subsequent evolution.[27] Just as the council fathers made Vatican II their own, so too the people of Latin America receive the Council and make it their own. Let us examine some of the basic perspectives of the Council and see how they have been creatively received by the Christian communities and their theology.

Vatican II made it clear that the world is not in the Church, the Church is in the world. The Church is the sacramental sign of the world's salvation and unity. Latin America asked itself, In what world does the Church most wish to be as sacrament of salvation? And it answered, In the world of the poor—in the underworld of the vast masses of our people.

Vatican II speaks repeatedly of the "mystery of salvation." In Latin America this salvation has been seen, concretely, in the process of integral liberation in its various mediations—economic (liberation from hunger), political (liberation from marginalization), cultural (liberation from illiteracy and ignorance), pedagogical (liberation from depersonalizing dependency), and religious (liberation from sin as rejection of God and God's historical project).

Vatican II speaks of "human promotion." Here in Latin America, *human promotion* has been concretely translated as "the liberation of the oppressed."

The Council spoke of the poverty of the world and of the poor. Here in Latin America, poverty has received a political content. Poverty is not innocent or natural. Poverty is the product of economic and sociopolitical mechanisms. It is not enough to condemn poverty as a moral evil. It is a matter of urgency to defeat it politically, through some other manner of organizing society, so that our society will be marked by fewer disparities and social injustices.

In speaking of salvation history, Vatican II also refers to a history of perdition, and a "sin of the world." In Latin America this sin of the world has been specified as social, structural sin. Concretely, the sin of the world consists in systems, structures, and social conventions that generate attitudes, practices, and consequences contradicting the will of God and wronging our sisters and brothers.

The Council plumbed the mystery of the Church, understanding *Church* primarily as the people of God *in via,* God's people on a journey, on the march. Now, in Latin America, the "people" are both Christian and poor. Concretely, then, the people of God in Latin America are made up, in their immense majority, of the poor. The Church as people of God, then, means the Church of the poor, understanding *poor* in its direct, empirical sense. The rest of Christians, who are not poor, have the duty to align themselves with the poor, and thus to incorporate themselves into the historical people of God who presently actualize the reality of the Suffering Servant.

Vatican II placed enormous emphasis on the mission of the Church. In a way, the Council did its reflection on the entire ecclesial mystery from a point of departure in the mission of the Son and the Spirit as prolonged in the mission of the Church, that sign and instrument of the salvation universally offered by God to all men and women. In Latin America the mission of the Church is defined in a particular way as a commitment to the liberation of the oppressed. Only by transforming the reality of evil into good can the Church signify the Good News of Jesus Christ.

The year 1968 saw the Second General Conference of the Council of Latin American Bishops, or CELAM, at Medellín in Colombia. All of the labors of that assembly were performed under the sign, "the Church in the current transformation of Latin America in the light of the Council." The concerns of Christians committed to the transformation of society, and the serious reflection accompanying these concerns, echoed mightily in the work of the bishops at Medellín. It would be fair to say that the prevailing theology of this celebrated conference was the one already beginning to be referred to as the theology of liberation. The methodology taken up by Medellín was definitely that of liberation theology. This methodology had been born of the Jocist, or Young Christian Worker, movement, and had become classic in the principal documents of various Latin American episcopates. The method unfolds in three steps. Its point of departure is always an observation of the practices of Christians and a critical analysis of reality. This first step is called the moment of seeing. Next comes the moment of judgment, in which an attempt is made to illuminate the practices observed in the first moment by examining them under the lens of revelation by means of a theological reflection. Third and last, courses of pastoral activity are charted, in what is called the moment of action.

In the course of the Medellín conference, however, the CELAM bishops reversed the perspective from which they had originally proposed to work. Instead of dealing with the transformation of Latin American life in the light of the Council, simply applying the teaching of the Second Vatican Council to Latin American reality, they sought to enrich the conciliar doctrine itself from a point of departure in the reality of the poor and oppressed of our continent.[28] The bishops and their *periti* had intended no such change of outlook. The latter simply imposed itself from the moment the assembled bishops and theologians sought to be faithful both to the reality of a suffering people and to the Gospel. The Medellín documents all speak from a stance favoring "the liberation of the entire human being and all human beings" (Document on Youth, no. 15). The texts emphasize that the divine deed of salvation consists in human beings' integral liberation (Justice, no. 4). "Christ . . . focused his mission around proclaiming the liberation of the poor" (Poverty, no. 7).[29] Religious education, then, must be impregnated with the concept of liberation (Religious Education, no. 6); all education must be capable of "delivering us human beings from our cultural, economic, and political servitude (Education, no. 7).

After Medellín the theology of liberation blossomed throughout nearly all of Latin America. Its inaugural theoretical formulation appeared in December 1971, with the publication of Gustavo Gutiérrez's *Theology of Liberation: History, Politics and Salvation.*[30] May of the same year had seen the appearance of Hugo Assmann's *Opresión-liberación: desafío a los cristianos.*[31] In July 1972, *Jesus Christ Liberator: A Critical Christology for Our Time* was published.[32] This is not the place to trace the history of the development of the theology of liberation from the intuitions of Vatican II. Suffice it to note that the years following Medellín were marked by a gradually intensifying and more consistent shift in the focus of the Latin American Church from center to periphery.[33] Base church communities sprang up by the thousands throughout the continent. The people reclaimed the Bible as their own, and formed thousands of study groups to examine it.

Beginning in 1968 highly repressive military governments have been installed in nearly all of the countries of Latin America. Since then the Christian communities have known only repression, arrest, torture, and martyrdom, right in their villages. Hundreds of laity and religious, as well as a goodly number of priests, have been expelled from their countries. Others have been tortured. Some have been murdered. Not even bishops have been spared.

This context has inspired a reflection from a perspective of captivity. The theology of captivity is not, despite the allegation of its critics, put forward as an alternative to liberation theology. The latter is always done against a backdrop of oppression and captivity.[34] A specific theology of captivity only seeks to accentuate the modification of the political conjuncture that has now been introduced through the systematic repression of any alternative movement on the part of the people and the Church or any organs of civil society. This context also provides the matrix of a vigorous critique by the Church of the national security doctrine. For the proponents of the national security doctrine, politics is total war, on an ongoing basis. The term *national security* masks international capitalism's strategic concern to defend itself through the coercive power of the states of the periphery and their organs of information and repression. International capitalism and its Latin American regimes cannot abide a society conscientized and organized to demand structural changes. Here the Church becomes the vicarious platform of all domesticated, if not outright suppressed, civil entities. The Church in Latin America is the voice of a people that has altogether lost *vez e voz*—participation and voice.

Here it has been the bishops conferences of Brazil and (particularly) Chile that have developed the most effective pastoral ministry for the defense and promotion of human rights. The bishops use the international press to denounce the torture of political prisoners and the abduction and "disappearance" of thousands of militant members of populist political parties and unions—or anyone at all deemed involved in resistance to the mechanisms of oppression of a military, authoritarian state.[35]

In a like atmosphere of totalitarian control of public life, the base church communities acquire enormous social and political relevance.[36] In the shadow of the hierarchy, this is the only "free space" for the people to meet. They gather around the Word of God, but in the light of that Word they discuss their problems and make their denunciations. Humbly but forthrightly, they voice their prophetic critique of the prevailing system of domination. The Church discharges a priceless political *diakonia* here. Non-believers, too, participate in the base community meetings, to maintain some minimum of contact with the people, and they come in numbers. The communities insist, however, that their religious and ecclesial nature be respected at all times.

FIVE PASTORAL THEOLOGY GUIDELINES FOR A CHURCH IN STEP WITH THE POOR

In the years from Medellín (1968) to Puebla (1979), in the Latin American Church, and more particularly in the vast episcopacy of Brazil (which has more than 350 bishops), five great pastoral guidelines were drawn up, crystallizing a practice and a reflection structured within the vision of the theology of liberation.

The first pastoral guideline in our land is a *preferential option for the poor*. We make an option for the poor against their poverty.[37] This implies a shift in the primary social locus from which the Church has traditionally sought to be constituted. Our Latin American people are made up overwhelmingly of the poor. Some 80 percent of them fall into this category. And our Latin American people are Christian.

Of course the Church had always existed *for* the poor. It had maintained a Herculean work of aid and assistance among them for centuries. But it had never been concerned to take advantage of the "power of the poor in history." The Church had belonged to the hegemonical historical bloc that conducted society in Latin America in the most elitist manner imaginable. Then, with the mobilization of the popular classes beginning in the 1930s, the

Church, via an engaged pastoral approach on the part of a significant cross section of its leaders, began to be *with* the poor.

Now, with the preferential option for the poor, the Church means to be a Church *of* the poor. This preferential option must be correctly understood. First of all, it is the hierarchy that makes this option. It is by this means that the hierarchy seeks to insert itself into the world of the poor. Priest, bishop, and lay minister are now more simple, naked, evangelical. Next, the poor themselves begin to assume a more direct participation in the life of the Church. They take on pastoral functions, help determine the avenues of a popular pastoral approach, and generally assist in the creation of a new way of being laity. From this convergence of hierarchical and lay renovation, a new shape of Church, one that is more *communio* and *diakonia* than society and hierarchy, is gradually being born.

The "poor" referred to as the objects of this preferential option are the oppressed popular classes. Poverty is the by-product of "determinate situations and economic, social, and political structures" (Puebla, no. 30).[38] These structures constitute social and structural sin. No one may hold aloof from this option. All must make it, cardinals, rich, poor, all. For the rich an option for the poor means taking up the cause of the poor, which is the actualization of social justice through profound structural transformations of society. For the poor an option for the poor means making an option for the very poorest, and joining together with other poor in order to seek, together, what all most lack in terms of a life of justice and dignity in a communion of sisters and brothers.

The option for the poor is *preferential.* The Church never forgets the catholicity of the faith. It opts for the poor, then, not in sectarian fashion, as if it opted only for the poor, to the exclusion of all others, but in such wise as simultaneously to remain open to all other social classes as well. Not that *preferential* is a synonym for *more* or *special*—as when, let us say, a mother loves all of her children, surely, but prefers the one who is ill. The sense of *preferential* in our case is more radical, and stems from an analysis of the generative causes of social poverty. The poor are not an island.

They exist in relation to the exploitative rich, both directly and through allies outside the wealthy classes who support them in their struggle. There is a causal relationship between wealth and poverty. To make a preferential option for the poor, then, means to love primarily the poor, as Jesus does—and then, starting with the poor, to love everyone, calling all of the others to deliver themselves from the mechanisms that produce the wealth of some and the poverty of others. Physicians love their patients when they combat the causes of their maladies. The Church loves the poor in combating not the persons of the rich, but the socioeconomic mechanisms that make the rich wealthy at the expense of the poor.

The second guideline, one intimately bound up with the first, is that a pastoral approach must always be made in terms of *integral liberation.* [39] An option is made for the persons and organizations of the poor and against their poverty. Now, it is the whole, or "integral" personhood of the poor that is envisaged in this option. Liberation, as we have seen, implies a practical, social, and political activity that aims to enlarge the space of freedom of the poor. An integral liberation is an economic, political, and pedagogical liberation, too, and not only a spiritual one, not only liberation from sin, not only a deliverance from the impulses of hatred and revenge. We regard this popular process as a way of anticipating and concretizing the good things of the Kingdom in the unity of the poor, in the quest of the poor for participation in public life, in social justice, and in loving, egalitarian relationships. In practice the official discourse of many Latin American national bishops conferences centers on the liberative Gospel, and an ecclesial action calculated to fan the flames of liberation by conferring on the liberation process the transcendent dimension it enjoys in the perspective of faith, however concretely it may be identified with the historical actualization of the design of God—the Reign *in fieri,* the Reign *in via.*

A third guideline used in our pastoral ministry comes to expression in the *base church communities.* The grass roots communities are more than an instrument of parish action, more than a tool of a pastoral strategy that has undergone Vatican II's *aggiornamento.* Our communities are our concrete translation of what the Council means by the Church's evangelization in the midst of the poor. The base communities are the Church at the grass roots. *Base,* then—*de base*—has three meanings: First, the persons at the base are those in the lowest echelons of society, the poor, the laborer, the marginalized. *Base* also means the small, basic group in which the primary, nominal relations originate. Finally, *base* refers to a pedagogical process that works "from the bottom up," in which the authorities, the teachers, listen to the people, discuss with them the pilgrim journey of the Church, and supervise the implementation of decisions made jointly with them, so that these decisions may be fruitful everywhere, from these groups "on the bottom" all the way to the "top," where we see the vehicles of sacred power.

The basic church communities represent a genuine "ecclesiogenesis," a birth of the Church, deep within the faith of a people in poverty. Here are a people who concretize the Church as an event of the Spirit—that event that occurs when the faithful meet in community, under a shade tree, to reflect on the Word of God and its light in order to confront the problems of the group. Then, within this Church born of the people, various ministries and services emerge, different forms of celebrations of faith materialize. The Gospel is interwoven with life. The basic church communities remold the figures of bishop and priest, religious and layperson, and especially woman. It is in the base community that the people exercise their way of being free. It is here that they are organizing for liberation from their very concrete oppressions, with an evangelical *parrhesia*—confidence and liberty—to exercise a humble propheticism against the social system and its agents of oppression. And the basic communities, once evangelized, evangelize the entire Church. It is they who are principally responsible for the evangelization of bishops, indeed for the genuine conversion of cardinals and bishops, priests and theologians.

The fourth guideline of our pastoral theology centers on the theme of *human rights.* The national bishops conferences of Latin

America have become the mouthpiece of the victims of political torture all throughout our lands. In a wide variety of sectors over the past several years, centers for the defense of human rights, along with justice and peace commissions, have sprung up everywhere. In Brazil there are more than a hundred centers on the popular level alone. Here the cause of human rights is fostered in a nonbourgeois version. The rights of the poor are spoken of as the rights of God (cf. Puebla, nos. 1217, 1228). The rights in question are prioritized: first come the right to life and the means of life—food, health, housing, employment, education—then the classic rights celebrated and advanced over the past two centuries, such as freedom of conscience and opinion, freedom of religion and worship. The whole pastoral activity of the Church in our countries encourages the promotion of peace and justice via an increased participation on the part of the poor at all levels of society and Church.

Finally, a fifth guideline of our pastoral activity emphasizes an *option for youth.* Young people—persons under eighteen years of age—make up more than one-half of the Latin American population. But the majority of our youth are condemned to live their lives without ever having been young. At the first possible moment, they are absorbed into the productive process under conditions of exploitation that are possible only because the victims are young. Our pastoral activity with our youth aims basically at making them agents of change in society—not by way of violence, but through the liberation process, in solidarity with an organized people.

THE THEOLOGY OF LIBERATION AS A THIRD WORLD EXPRESSION

Our pastoral practice has been steadily accompanied by a rich theological reflection in the framework of the theology of liberation. In the years between Medellín (1968) and Puebla (1979), a spirituality of liberation took root in our lands. We perceived the importance of a liberative pedagogy of the oppressed, and we assimilated this approach in our religious education. We reread the history of the Church in Latin America from the perspective of the victims of colonial evangelization—our Amerindians, blacks, and mestizos. Of course, we are well aware that, in the very midst of a theology of domination, elements of a prophetic liberative theology have never been lacking. First there was a Montesinos, a Las Casas, a Vieira. Then came the era of the national emancipation struggles, and we had a Morelos and a Frei Caneca. Finally, with the crises of the developmentalistic models, from 1960 onward,[40] liberation theology itself has consolidated its methodology and, especially, has developed its Christology and ecclesiology.

During recent years our reflection on the liberation theme has been channeled through a framework of reflection on the actual, concrete practices maintained by Christians. Thereby we sound out the potential of a popular Catholicism for resistance to domination and for the liberation of the poor. Now we have a genuine theology of life, one that militates against the mechanisms of a capitalist system that generates the deaths of so many millions of victims of all sorts of exploitation. We have a theology of the land, on a continent where millions of Latin Americans are driven from their little plots to wander in search of a small piece of land where they can live and work. We have a theology of dominated cultures and races, such as our indigenous peoples and our blacks, who are beginning to appreciate their right to appropriate the Gospel, inserting it within the various frameworks of their perceptions of the world.

The message must needs take flesh. True, all of this pastoral effervescence in the Church, from foundation to cupola, has aroused fear in certain segments of the hierarchy, as well in some of the power strata in civil society. There is no dearth of those who combat this theology, accusing it of Marxist tendencies and of seeking to politicize the faith in order to change society. Indeed, there have even been instances in which conservative church groups in Latin America have entered into a veritable conspiracy with their European counterparts to thwart this development in our pastoral ministry and theological reflection. Notwithstanding all obstacles, however, the liberation perspective is gradually acquiring more definite contours. International conferences are bearing fruit in Africa and Asia.[41] Today the theology of liberation, in various forms, is the theology of the poor, peripheral churches of the whole Third World. These expressions of liberation theology all represent a creative reception of the intuitions and urgings of the Second Vatican Council.

In Africa the impact of liberation theology is on autochthonous cultures maintained in a state of captivity by the dominant cultures of ex-colonists or their native allies. In Asia the great religions have come into the arena of discussion. How can the latter be reread in such a way that, with all respect for their religious nature, they become a factor in the liberation of the poor and of these great cultures of silence? In Latin America the challenge is the social injustice suffered by our impoverished, religious masses. Every vector of the theology of liberation aims at the same objective: the gestation of more space for that supreme gift of God's Reign, freedom.[42]

Not once are the words *liberation theology* mentioned in the final document redacted at Puebla at CELAM's Third General Conference. Enormous pressure was brought to bear on the synodal fathers not to use that term. But liberation theology's basic intuitions, along with the liberation theme itself, are everywhere. First of all, the lengthy document is entirely structured according to liberation theology's methodological framework. The text opens with an analysis of Latin American society and its aspirations, together with an examination of the social practice of Christians and others in that society. In other words, it begins with the moment of seeing. Then it engages in a theological reflection on this pastoral reading of reality, expounding its Christology, anthropology, and ecclesiology in this context—the moment of judgment. Finally, it plots practical courses of action for Church and society, in an effort to concretize human liberation from a point of departure that is at the heart of an oppressed society—the moment of action.

Most important, however, Puebla adopted and consecrated the central theme of the theology of liberation: the preferential option for the poor, "understood as solidarity with the poor and as a rejection of the situation in which most people on this continent live" (Puebla, no. 1156). Indeed, the proclamation of integral liberation "belongs to the very core of . . . evangelization" (no. 480). This proclamation is an indispensable, essential, integral part of the very mission of the Church (cf. nos. 355, 476, 480, 1254, 1283, 1302). "This liberation is gradually being realized in history" (no. 483), and it also opens out integrally upon a transcendent dimension (no. 475). The bishops of Latin America acknowledge that "the best service to our fellows is evangelization, which disposes them to fulfill themselves as children of God, liberates them from injustices, and fosters their integral advancement" (no. 1145).

THE CHANCE FOR A CHRISTIANITY OF THE POOR

The reception of the Second Vatican Council, sprung from the anxieties and aspirations of the poor, has endowed the conciliar message with an evangelical concretion. Suddenly there is a chance for all Christianity to think itself and build itself from a point of departure deep among the condemned of the Earth. The poor have always found a merciful welcome, and a place of their own, in the Church. But they have never been accorded a collective status as principal historical subject of the effectuation of the project of the Poor One of Nazareth. Now they are emerging in history with their demand for profound changes. They are bursting into the Church with their evangelization, showing us that it is theirs to assume the privileged position accorded by the God of the Old Testament to the slaves of Egypt and the captives of Babylon, the position defined by Jesus from the very beginning of his proclamation of his Good News. In short, theirs is the place of the poor in the Reign of God. Our partiality toward the poor is the concrete realization of the universality of the Gospel. None can be indifferent to the poor. The poor embrace the cause of their poor sisters and brothers, the rich take up the cause of justice and participation for the oppressed. Thus all feel the same concern, and all open themselves to the real possibility of a catholic concretization of the Christian faith.

The theology emerging from this process of gestation of a new kind of Christian offers us a new paradigm for theology. Here we have a reflection on social reality, especially from the viewpoint of the poor, in the light of the Word of Revelation and the practice of Jesus of Nazareth and his Apostles. Suddenly a theologian is more than just a teacher, a professor. Theologians are militants, Christian intellectuals organically involved with the historical movement of the poor, their thinking, speaking, writing, and action all incorporated into the messianic struggle of "the ones who have survived the great period of trial" (Rev. 7:14). They will count themselves blessed if their discourse in quest of the interconnections of the Word of God with the course of the history of the oppressed generates meaning, *joi de vivre,* and an apostolic *parrhesia.* Then gladly will they spend their lives and intellectual energies on behalf of those who actualize for us the passion of the Suffering Servant, as we share with them their journey through history toward the Reign of God.[43]

2. Mission of the Church in Latin America: To Be the Good Samaritan

The mission of the Church is to evangelize. Two principal concretizations enflesh the evangelizing practice: prophecy and pastoral ministry. In its prophecy the Church is judge, in the light of the revealed Word, of the sociohistorical reality into which it is inserted. The Church proclaims God's design, and denounces anything that opposes that design. In its pastoral ministry the Church animates the Christian life, coordinates the various tasks incumbent on the Christian, creates the vital synthesis between Gospel and life, and joyfully celebrates the presence of the grace that sets men and women free.

In the following considerations I will emphasize the pastoral aspect of the Church's mission of evangelization. I will also take care not to neglect the prophetic moment that is always part of the animation of Christian life. Let us begin with one of Jesus' parables.

Jesus has given us the story of the Good Samaritan.[1] In extremely concrete terms this parable paints the ideal picture of the mission of the Church in Latin America.[2] The mission of the Church is always to serve human beings, especially those who, like the victim in the parable, have fallen and are "half-dead" (Luke 10:30). This was Jesus' mission as well. This was the mission of the Son of God: to liberate the oppressed (Luke 4:17–21, 7:23; Matt. 9:35; Mark 7:37; Acts 10:38), to heal the sick (Luke 5:26), and to forgive sinners (Matt. 9:13). Jesus came to serve (Matt. 20:28). He came that we might have life, and might have it in abundance (John 10:10). The Church finds the meaning of its existence in the prolongation of Jesus' service to all women and men, particularly to the humiliated and the offended of our history.

The parable of the Good Samaritan shows us the starting point for thinking and living our mission. That starting point is not the Church. The starting point is our neighbor, the distant one. In the imagery of the parable, our mission begins with those who, as we see, have fallen prey to robbers (Luke 10:30). The mission of the Church is to make of the ones far away our neighbors, of our neighbors our brothers and sisters, and of our brothers and sisters the sons and daughters of God.

If, in order to define mission, we start with ourself, we shall be like the Pharisee in the parable. We shall begin by asking, "And who is *my* neighbor?" (Luke 10:29). Whom shall I love and whom not? Mission, in these terms, is only an extension of oneself. It fails to actualize the Abrahamic experience of emergence from oneself in order to move toward the other as other.

Jesus turns the question around. Jesus asks not Who is my neighbor? but Who is the neighbor of the fallen one? Who is neighbor to the victim of oppression? Jesus' definition of mission begins with the wounded, half-dead victim. Who is the neighbor of the *other*, the one fallen by the side of the road (Luke 10:36)? The answer: the one who approaches that victim "with compassion" (Luke 10:37). The neighbor, then, is someone who has burst the bonds of self and stooped, bent down toward the abandoned other. In the parable the neighbor was the Good Samaritan. Now, Samaritans were regarded by Jesus' people not as "good" at all, but as heretics. From that time forward, however, the Samaritan has always had the epithet *Good,* despite not belonging to the ranks of orthodoxy as represented by the priest and the Levite, orthodoxy that failed to fulfill the most important element of the law: mercy (Matt. 23:23).

For Jesus, my neighbor is anyone to whom I draw near. And I ought to draw near to all women and men, particularly my enemies (Matt. 5:44) and the poor and the plundered whom I meet along the pathway of my journey on Earth. "Go and do the same," Jesus enjoins us (Luke 10:37).

LATIN AMERICA, CONTINENT STRIPPED NAKED: CHALLENGE TO THE MISSION OF THE CHURCH

How does the Church accomplish its mission to be Latin America's Good Samaritan?

The Latin American continent lives its life in the same condition as the victim in Jesus' parable. Since its very discovery it has been dependent on others, who strip it, do it violence, and leave it half-dead (Luke 10:30).[3] In 1552 Bartolomé de las Casas wrote of this issue, describing the two fundamental behaviors of the colonists in his *Very Brief Account of the Destruction of the Indies.*[4] The first, he says, consists in unjust, cruel, sanguinary, and tyrannical wars. The second follows the same logic of violence. Here is oppression of human beings under the harshest, most horrible and wretched servitude to which humans or animals could be subjected. We have a long account of the injustice and mistreatment inflicted on our indigenous civilizations from the pen of Dominican Juan Ramírez, bishop of Guatemala (1601–60). Before naming the seventeen forms of violence used by the colonists in his jurisdiction, he warns us that they are of such an order "that neither the Grand Turk nor the Moorish King would have inflicted them on their Christian enemies in Constantinople."[5] During the years of the Council of Trent (1545–63), the great, irreplaceable civilizations of Central America and Mexico were so barbarously devastated that in the course of fifty years the population was reduced by nearly nine-tenths. It is calculated that in 1532 seventeen million Amerindian natives inhabited the territory of Mexico. Half a century later the figure was barely two million.[6] No Latin American bishop was allowed to participate in the Council of Trent: the church of Latin America was considered to be more the property of the Spanish crown than of Rome. The council fathers had not a word to say about the genocide being committed in our lands. Like so many of the theologians of the time, they saw no very great sin in it. After all, the people being eliminated were only pagans, such as the Aztecs who sacrificed other pagans to their sun god.

There are too many stations on the Latin American way of the cross even to summarize. I will only observe that colonialism has now been transformed into neocolonialism, so that the servitude of days gone by continues under other signs and other lords, and perdures to the present. In the words of the Latin American bishops gathered at Puebla:

From the depths of the countries that make up Latin America a cry is rising to heaven, growing louder and more alarming all the time. It is the cry of a suffering people who demand justice, freedom, and respect for the basic rights of human beings and peoples. . . . The cry . . . is loud and clear, increasing in volume and intensity, and at times full of menace. (Puebla Final Document, nos. 87, 89)[7]

As we see, an entire continent has fallen by the roadside, prey to centuries of plundering. Has the Church been its neighbor, its Good Samaritan? Surely it has embodied more than one of the figures in Jesus' parable. It has been the priest and the Levite, who passed by, callous accomplices of a criminal domination. As the bishops at Puebla acknowledge:

Not all of us in the Latin American Church have committed ourselves sufficiently to the poor. We are not always concerned about them, or in solidarity with them. Service to them really calls for constant conversion and purification. (Ibid., no. 1140)

But the Church has been the Good Samaritan too, and right from the beginning. Countless synods and provincial councils embodied the figure of the Good Samaritan, as at Lima and Mexico City, Santo Domingo and Santa Fé, Bogotá and La Plata, through countless bishops, such as Julián Gárcez (1528–42), Juan de Zumárraga (1528–48), Vasco de Quiroga (1538–65), Bartolomé de las Casas (1544–47), Antonio Valdivieso (1544–50), and Toribio de Mogrovejo (1581–1606), as well as through so many other theologians and missionaries, such as Anchieta and Vieira in

Brazil, José de Acosta in Peru, Bernardino de Sahagún in Mexico, and Antonio de Montesinos in Santo Domingo. Each was genuinely a neighbor to the stricken Latin American continent.[8]

Let us examine more closely the way in which the Church today seeks to carry out its mission of mercy and solidarity with the anguish and the hopes of the human being in Latin America.

PROPHETIC PROCLAMATION OF THE GOSPEL

The greatest service performed by the Church for the women and men of Latin America is the proclamation of the Gospel of Jesus Christ.[9] The Gospel, in turn, is nothing but the proclamation of the Reign of God: the full and total liberation of all creation, cosmic and human, from all its iniquities, and the integral accomplishment of God's design in the insertion of all things into his own divine life. Concretely, then, the Reign of God translates into community of life with the Father, the Son, and the Holy Spirit in a universal communion of brothers and sisters in solidarity with one another in the use of the "fruit of the earth and the work of human hands." This Good News is a grace of God, and we receive it gratefully. We attain to it when we change our life and place ourself in the discipleship of Jesus. Now, Jesus not only proclaimed the Reign of God. He concretized it in his life. He inaugurated the Reign in his words and deeds. His whole existence was self-surrender to others, and a courageous appeal for their conversion. As a result he met with obstacles and persecution. Rejected, he accepted martyrdom as the supreme witness of his fidelity to his Father and his love for human beings, especially for the poor, whom he considered the primary addressees of his proclamation of joy and hope (Luke 6:20). And his Resurrection has manifested the first of the ultimate fruits of the Reign of God: the first new human being (cf. 1 Cor. 15:45; Col. 3:10; Eph. 4:24) and the real possibility of "new heavens and a new earth" (Rev. 21:1).

All through his life Jesus joined the proclamation of the Reign, with its concrete anticipation in history, beginning with the integral salvation of the most forsaken (Luke 7:22). Analogously, the

Church, too, in its prolongation of the hope proclaimed by Jesus, actualizes that hope as well, in deeds of liberation from oppression, deeds of solidarity with the weak, deeds that reactivate all of the energies of a goodness capable of overcoming selfishness. The Gospel says explicitly, "As you go, make this announcement: 'The reign of God is at hand!' Cure the sick, raise the dead, heal the leprous, expel demons" (Matt. 10:7–8). Here, in a single breath, Jesus sets forth his concept of the unity that must obtain between the proclamation of the Reign and liberative action that builds that Reign. Jesus not only preaches, he takes pity on a hungry, wandering people, and feeds them to satiety with loaves and fishes (Luke 9:11–17; Mark 6:32–44).

Jesus' attitude in this regard constitutes the Church's paradigm for its activity as the Good Samaritan. The Church not only evangelizes by word, it helps transform the reality of evil into Good, in the light of the Gospel. Only thus is the Gospel the Good News of truth for women and men. Puebla repeats what Paul VI has said in *Evangelii Nuntiandi:*

The Church . . . has the duty to *proclaim the liberation* of millions of human beings, among whom are many of the Church's own children; the duty to help *bring this liberation forth* in the world, to bear witness to it and make sure that it is total. None of this is alien to evangelization. (Puebla Final Document, no. 26; citing Paul VI, *Evangelii Nuntiandi,* no. 30)

But we must be careful here. The Holy Father and the Conference of Bishops are not saying that the Church must simply produce liberation, after the fashion of a revolutionary movement or an agency of human promotion. No, the Church is to *help* in liberation. The actual agents of liberation are the oppressed themselves. As their consciousness is raised and they begin to organize, mobilizing to transform society in the direction of more justice and participation, the oppressed themselves become the agents of their own liberation. The Church, the Christian community, joins in this struggle, legitimates such and such a cause, making its specific contribution. Here, in the commitment to a liberative evangelization, the Church manifests the compassion of the Good Samaritan.

Let me present just three practices on the part of the Latin American church that concretize this approach.

1) Defense and promotion of a minimally decent standard of living
2) Defense and promotion of the rights of the poor
3) Reinvention of the Church at the grassroots as People of God in the midst of the Latin American poor

It may well be in points such as these that the originality of our churches exists. Well did Pope John Paul II say, in his encyclical *Dives in Misericordia,* that the true face of mercy must always be discovered anew. I think that the three approaches that I have just listed are a correct response to this papal plea.

DEFENSE AND PROMOTION OF A MINIMALLY DECENT STANDARD OF LIVING

Everyone knows the trouble with Latin American societies. Pope John Paul II identified it as "the ever increasing wealth of the rich at the expense of the ever increasing poverty of the poor."[10] The scandal for our religion is that the vast majority of the population are both Christian and poor. The rich say, "Lord, Lord," but they refuse to do the will of God (cf. Matt. 7:21), which is to foster the life of the human being. Rightly does the Second Vatican Council call "this split between the faith which many profess and their daily lives" one of the "more serious errors of our age" (*Gaudium et Spes,* no. 43).[11] The Council's observation is particularly valid with respect to the Christians of Latin America, who receive inadequate evangelization concerning the social and political responsibility of the faith (cf. Puebla Final Document, no. 515).

In the measure that the pastors have entered into the life of the people, they have shared the oppressions of these people—the repression of all movements on behalf of social change. They have had the experience that Jesus had when he said, "My heart is moved with pity for the crowd" (Mark 8:2). Profoundly, existentially, they have rediscovered the poor as Jesus' younger sisters and brothers (cf. Matt. 25:40),[12] whose life is in perpetual mortal danger from the situation in which they are forced to live. The mission of the Church is to help safeguard and promote a minimally humane and just life for all men and women, in terms of an integral conception of human life.[13] The Church should behave as did the father of the prodigal, in the parable so perceptively analyzed by Pope John Paul II in *Dives in Misericordia:* the mission of the Church is to save the humanity of human beings (no. 41; cf. no. 98). What really matters is human life. After all, it is human life, called to the communion of the divine life, that constitutes God's greatest sacrament. We are reminded of Bartolomé de las Casas's celebrated principle: "Better a live heathen Indian than a dead Christian one."[14] We find much the same thing in Mexico in 1577 with the Jesuit theologian José de Acosta and his treatise *De Procuranda Indorum Salute* ("Securing the Salvation of the Indians"). Evangelization is simply the prolongation of the practice of Jesus Christ. It should produce life, then, as Jesus did—that Jesus who is himself "the word of life . . . that . . . became visible to us" (1 John 1:1–2). The Christian God is a God of life, and a God who calls the dead to life (cf. Rom. 4:17). There is no genuine testimonial to the Christian God where at least a minimal degree of life is not defended and fostered. The great challenge to the Church in Latin America resides in its call to denounce the Latin American social system of death, and help in the gestation of a society calculated to generate a minimally human life for all, especially for the great impoverished masses.

The Church is aware of this challenge, and this consciousness has materialized in two great options: the preferential option for the poor, and the option for their integral liberation. Let us briefly examine these two options.

PREFERENTIAL OPTION FOR THE POOR: OPTION AGAINST SOCIAL INJUSTICE

The word *poor* in the expression "preferential option for the poor," must be understood in the sense in which it is used at Puebla. Puebla regards the reality of poverty as "the most devastating and humiliating kind of scourge" (Puebla Final Document, no. 29). Far from being "a passing phase," poverty is "the product of economic, social, and political situations and structures" (no. 30). The word *poor* has a concrete, historical sense, then, and not just a metaphorical, spiritual one. This is abundantly clear in the parable of the Good Samaritan, in which the traveler "fell among robbers," who "stripped him, beat him, and then went off leaving him half-dead" (Luke 10:30). Surely no one would maintain that the stripped and beaten victim in the parable was stripped and beaten only spiritually. Just so, when we say that the Church has made an option for the poor, we mean that it has made an option for those who are physically poor. Now, these poor have been rendered poor unjustly. They are impover*ished.* [15] They have fallen prey to robbers.

Entirely apart from faith, and the Gospel, this care of the poor possesses an intrinsic worth and dignity. The agent of this care of the poor may be a non-Christian, as the merciful doer of the will of God in the parable of the Good Samaritan was a Samaritan heretic. The succoring of the wounded—especially of a whole exploited social class assaulted in its life and dignity, such as we have in Latin America—involves the denunciation of a social injustice that produces poverty. It also involves a positive proclamation, a testimony on behalf of a minimally human life for all—especially for the half-dead.

But the Christian community has other reasons for making a preferential option for the poor, over and above this humanitarian consideration. First of all, the option is originally a divine one. The reason for the preference in question lies deep in the nature of God. God is a living God, a God of life and the giver of life. When someone's life is threatened, God takes that person's side to protect and promote that threatened life. A Church that defends life and helps create conditions in which life may flourish performs the liturgy that is most agreeable to God. "Choose life, then, that you and your descendants may live" (Deut. 30:19).

Second, the option in question is a "Jesuological" one. Pope John Paul II reminded us of that at Puebla, when he called Jesus' defense of human rights "primarily a commitment to those most in need."[16] The actualization of the Reign begins with the poor (Luke

6:20). A bishop who fails to be the *defensor et procurator pauperum* is false to an essential part of the practice of the Good Shepherd and Good Samaritan par excellence, Jesus Christ.

Finally, the preferential option for the poor is an apostolic option. From the very first days of Christian evangelization, the poor were the object of a special solicitude on the part of the Apostles and Paul (cf. Acts 3:44–45, 4:24; Gal. 2:10; Acts 11:29–30). The intent of including the adjective *preferential* is not only to safeguard the essential catholicity of the faith—its openness to all human beings—but also to establish a certain order of priority in the Church's care, compassion, and love. The Church is to love everyone indeed—but starting with the poor. The Church is to love the rich, who make their option for the poor and the cause of the poor, for their life and their justice. The Church is to love the poor, who make their option for those even poorer than themselves. Thus all see themselves concerned, and the apparent partiality of this preferential option merely opens routes to the concretization of universal Christian love.

In Brazil we have many beautiful examples of this option for the very poorest. Here is one of them. A concrete preferential option for the poor can result in the promotion of life in its most biblical sense. Some years ago the Tapirapé Indians, who live in the interior, were being exterminated by contact with the whites. They had no resistance to their diseases. And so they decided to have no more children, and simply die out as a tribe. Then, more than thirty years ago now, the Little Sisters of Jesus came to our country. They made the option for the most abandoned, and went to live among the Tapirapé. Their objective was to help the people to a self-awareness, to help them realize that they were who they were, and so lead them back to a love of life. At first the sisters lived outside the village. They entered it only to visit the natives and proclaim the Gospel. But later they joined them in their work in the forest and on the great rock plateau. Eventually the Tapirapé trusted them so completely that they adopted them as members of their tribe, and the Little Sisters moved into the village. Their disinterested service, their support for the cause of the natives against their exploitation at the hands of the landowners, filled the Tapirapé with courage. The Tapirapé began having children again. Today they are a strong tribe, and their village rings with the shouts of many happy children. The Gospel, as the experience of a communion of life, as a communion of sisters and brothers, brought the Tapirapé life's benediction again.

Let us see one more example of an option for the poor and the promotion of life in our country. This time we shall look in São Paulo. In order to deal with the unemployment and hunger currently devastating so many thousands of families in the slums here, the base church communities have set up Project Five–Two. Jesus fed the hungry people with five loaves and two fishes (Mark 6:30–44 and parallels), and it is this gospel miracle that has given the project its name. Five families who are not suffering from unemployment band together and commit themselves to distribute basic foodstuffs to two families whose breadwinners are out of work. Again we have an actualization of the parable of the Good Samaritan, this time in the conditions of a modern industrial city.

OPTION FOR THE INTEGRAL LIBERATION OF THE POOR

The only genuine option for the poor is made by those who fight the poverty of the poor, which "the Church sees as a situation of social sinfulness" (Puebla Final Document, no. 28). First, in the struggles of the poor to transform their situation, the Church discerns the presence of the marks of the Reign of God, despite the possible presence of distortions, even sin. The Church sees that what the poor are striving for is more participation in social and political life, relationships of greater justice and solidarity. Second, the Church extracts from the Bible—for example, from the account of the exodus from Egypt, or from the prophets' commitment to justice for the poor—and especially from the words and practice of Jesus, the whole of the Bible's liberative content. The Christian faith is not reducible to this dimension of social liberation. But this is the dimension that we emphasize, as it is here that faith comes to grips with the involvement of Christians with their poor sisters and brothers for the purpose of abolishing the persistent inhumane and inhuman situation in which the poor are compelled to live.

Christian liberation is an open process, involving the whole human being. This is why it is called *integral.* It is not only spiritual, then. It is not only liberation from the overt sin that separates us from God. Liberation is economic, political, social, and pedagogical as well.[17] Grace can occur in these dimensions, and when it does, the Reign is concretized historically. But sin can occur in these dimensions, too—when elements contrary to the meaning of history and the project of God are present (Puebla Final Document, nos. 483, 515). In their commitment to integral liberation, Christians take up the instruments of an oppressed people's deliverance—unions, neighborhood associations, movements for the defense of the people in the slums, groups devoted to reflection and social action. The Church itself, in the national bishops conferences, has created organs whose direct purpose is the support and defense of the poor. In Brazil, for example, we have some particularly efficient groups, such as the Rural Ministry Commission, the Native Mission Council, the Justice and Peace Commission, Black Union and Awareness—bodies that defend not the corporate interests of the Church, but the interests of the poor.

The commitment of our Latin American Church to liberation has won it calumny, persecution (including persecution by conservative bishops), and the torture of a great number of its members. We have innumerable martyrs, among them archbishops Romero and Angelelli, to say nothing of priests, religious, and laity. The beatitude of persecution is an unmistakable sign of the evangelical character and truth of this attitude on the part of Christians.[18]

DEFENSE AND PROMOTION OF THE RIGHTS OF THE POOR

Modern democratic societies are founded on the acknowledgment of the rights and dignity of the human person. Because its matrix is in a laissez-faire economy, however, these rights are conceived and lived individualistically, without adequate regard for social responsibility. The rights that come in for the most emphasis are the ones that are of direct interest to the privileged strata of society: freedom of thought and expression, freedom of religion, the right to private property. In Latin America, under the national security regimes, in the name of the right to private property, that is, in the name of capital, all other rights are systematically violated: freedom of assembly, freedom of partisan political organization, freedom of the press and communication. In practically all of the countries of Latin America, the churches have assumed a prophetic role, lending their voices to those who have *nem voz nem vez,* neither voice nor their "turn"—no opportunity of participating in social or political life. Now torture, the "disappearances," and political murder are denounced for what they are. As Puebla acknowledges, the battle for human rights "may well be the original imperative of this divine hour on our continent" (Puebla Final Document, no. 320), constituting as it does an "integral part" of all evangelization (nos. 1254, 1283).

But its preferential option for solidarity with the poor has also led the Church to prioritize certain human rights over others. The first and primary rights to be protected and guarded are those of the great impoverished masses.[19] The commitment to the rights of all, then, must begin with a commitment to the basic rights that regard primarily the poor: the right to life and the right to the means of life, such as health, employment, housing, education, and social security. Then, from a starting point in these fundamental rights, the Church promotes and defends the other basic human rights, such as politico-cultural and religious rights. The "Declaration on Human Rights and Reconciliation" of the Third General Assembly of the Synod of Bishops, which assembly was devoted to evangelization (1972), makes such a prioritization.[20]

In Latin America we speak of the "rights of the poor," as indeed we must, and the expression is taken over by the Puebla document (nos. 1217, 1119, 711, 324, 320). This approach to a recognition of human dignity and to a confrontation with its problems—an approach that begins with the plight of those who have fallen by the roadside—recovers the biblical perspective. In the Bible the rights of the poor are equivalated with the rights of God:

He who oppresses the poor blasphemes his Maker, but he who is kind to the needy glorifies him.

Prov. 14:31; cf. 17:5

[God] executes justice for the orphan and the widow, and befriends the alien, feeding and clothing him.

Deut. 10:18; cf. Jer. 22:16

Those who do all of this for the poor do it for Jesus. Those who fail to do this have left Jesus in the lurch (Matt. 25:40, 45).

Our new awareness of the rights of the poor as the rights of God has led to the foundation, all over Latin America, of centers for the Defense of Human Rights and of Justice and Peace commissions. Particularly well known are the Vicariate for Solidarity, in Chile; the Peace and Justice Commission of Argentina, with its Nobel laureate Adolfo Pérez Esquivel; and CLAMOR ("Outcry"), or Commission for the Defense of Human Rights in the Southern Cone, based in São Paulo. CLAMOR, under the patronage of the great apostle of human rights Cardinal Paulo Evaristo Arns, conducted a long and dangerous investigation which ultimately identified 7291 of Argentina's disappeared. The list of those names, with full documentation, was handed over by Cardinal Arns to Pope John Paul II, who thereupon lodged a protest with the Argentine government.[21] In Brazil there are currently more than 150 popular organizations, centers, or commissions for the defense and promotion of human rights. As of this writing, two national congresses have already been held. Documentation published in Brazil recounts the struggle of the humble to become the Samaritans of the humiliated, despite all manner of threats, persecutions, even torture and murder.[22] But Christians here have a perfect grasp of the teaching of the 1974 Synod of Bishops, held in Rome: "The promotion of human rights is a demand of the gospel, and must occupy a central place in the ministry of the Church."

REINVENTION OF THE CHURCH AT THE GRASS ROOTS AS PEOPLE OF GOD IN THE MIDST OF THE LATIN AMERICAN POOR

One of the most original expressions of the faith lived by the people of Latin America is the emergence of thousands of base ecclesial communities all over the continent.[23] The base communities are more than extensions of traditional church institutions, like the parish or the pious association. They signify the presence of the entire Church at the base, or the grassroots. They *are* the whole Church, the Church among a poor and lowly people. When the hierarchical Church penetrates the Christian people—and permits this Christian people to penetrate itself, participating in liturgy, taking up the pastoral mission, making themselves coresponsible for the task of the Church via new lay ministries—then the whole-Church-as-People-of-God emerges. We should scarcely be surprised, then, to see the Church at the base composed not only of laity, but of cardinals, bishops, priests, and religious as well. Bishops learn by becoming the brothers of the sisters and brothers in the base community, and laity rise to a new dignity as they see themselves become their pastors' brothers and sisters in deed as well as word. The base church communities, involving as they do all of the members of the Church, with their specific differentiations, permit a recovery and actualization of the reality of the Church as communion of the faithful, *communitas fidelium*. This is the oldest and most theologically correct concept of Church. The Church has existed since the time of Jesus, but it always stands in need of being reinvented. It is not a lifeless organization two thousand years old, it is an organism. It grows, it renews and repairs itself, in proportion to its penetration of history and its response to new challenges. In Latin America, through the base communities, faith makes a collective response to the great challenges issuing from poverty and oppression.

Within these communities the individual becomes a Good Samaritan to someone else. These communities are the scene of a hand-to-hand combat: the battle to generate a life minimally worth living, the struggle to promote and defend, in community fashion, the rights of the human person, especially the impoverished human person. Almost naturally, the base community facilitates the unification of faith and life, of Gospel and liberation. Individuals deposit in the common store not only their faith and hope, but, even more, their lives, their oppressions, and their victories, always in the light of the word of revelation.

Then, as community, the base group performs a *diakonia* vis-à-vis the larger human community. In the slums of the city outskirts, in the hinterland, where the benefits of civilization are all but unknown, where might makes right, the base communities are frequently the people's sole collective, organized defense. It is they who stand up for peasants threatened with eviction from the land that is rightfully theirs, it is they who defend our Native Americans from the greed of the mighty capitalist projects, it is they who throw up crucial resistance to the violence of the police in the service of the mighty.

Recently this Church at the base has been accused of verging on being a "parallel church"—a "church" no longer in communion with the hierarchy. The base Church has been stigmatized as a "popular church" in a pejorative sense. But we simply endorse the humble, courageous response of the Christians of Nicaragua when faced with the same accusation. We're not the ones who call it a popular church, said the Nicaraguans. We just call ourselves Church. It is others who slap the "popular" label on us, so that in the next breath they can say we aren't the Christian Church. But we never use this name ourselves.[24] Indeed, as Paul VI declared, the Church at the base represents a "hope for the Church universal." Here is born the new Christian, the citizen of an earthly city modeled after the heavenly one, the new, collective Samaritan bending over the fallen victims of a life of oppression and assisting them to liberate themselves and to live more humanely and humanly.[25]

THE GOOD SAMARITAN IS ALIVE AND WELL AND LIVING IN BAHIA

Limpanzol is a region in the interior of Bahia. The shepherd is a Matthias Schmidt, a fine Benedictine bishop. Like other regions of Brazil, Limpanzol is the scene of many a battle for the land, as the large landholders evict the rightful owners. One day in 1981 nineteen farm workers from Colônia and Rumo (two hamlets of the hacienda) were abducted by police, at the behest of the landholders, transported to a distant hacienda, and herded into a corral like cattle. There they remained for two days, while the landholders and their police henchmen held a "victory" barbecue! The rightful owners, the farm workers themselves, had been unwilling to leave the little plots where they had lived and worked for so many years, and now the police and large landholders had evicted them by main force! What a feat! And so there had to be a celebration. Overcome with magnanimity, the revelers actually sent their women to the corral with servings for the prisoners—who politely refused to have any part in the travesty.

In the course of the "celebration," one of the victors, a certain Dr. Sebastião, a physician, ridiculed the nobility of the prisoners in refusing the meal they had been offered: "What! These gentlemen are being nice to you! They've sent their wives and daughters out to serve you a barbecue! If it'd been up to me, I'd have had you filled with the lead of a machine gun." At last the workers were released.

As they made their way home, in the dark of night, they came upon a stalled pickup by the side of the road. And there in the dark, someone was asking for help.

It was Dr. Sebastião. It was the gentleman who would have liked to have seen the farm workers cut down by a machine gun. The workers recognized him at once.

What was their reaction? We might think it would have been, "Ha! Now we shall have our revenge! Let's just let him sit out here tonight."

But that was not what the farm workers had learned in their base community. And so instead, their train of thought was, When we read the word of God and meditate on it, isn't one of the things we see that Jesus tells us is to love our enemies, to do good to those who hate us, and to be merciful, as our heavenly Father is merciful (Luke 6:27–36)? And doesn't St. Paul teach the same—"Never repay injury with injury. . . . Do not avenge yourselves. . . . Do not be conquered by evil but conquer evil with good" (Rom. 12:17–21)?

So the workers decided to help Dr. Sebastião. They helped him get his truck going again. They stopped along the deserted road to help the physician in need. The Good Samaritan was at his task again. Yes, he is still around. At that particular moment he came to life again in the Brazilian interior, in Bahia.

Happy the Church whose daughters and sons are Good Samaritans! Happy the Church for whom the parable is not only a parable, but who transform it into history, to liberate the fallen and the half-dead along the arduous roadway of the human journey to the divine Reign of life and communion.

3. Rights of the Poor: Rights of God

When we reflect on the modern history of human rights, we are perplexed and pained at the absence of the Church from that movement. The ferment for human rights has emerged in the world not only apart from, but, often enough, against, the Church. Modern society's rising consciousness with respect to human rights, together with its implementation of those rights, is scarcely divorced from the intuitions with which the Gospel has impregnated our culture; but where the church institution is concerned, we must face the fact of such condemnations in the past century as *Mirari Vos* under Gregory XVI and, especially, *Quanta Cura* and the *Syllabus of Errors* under Pius IX.

Practically everything the Western world regards as a basic human right today was once rejected by the official Church. Freedom of conscience was called an "erroneous opinion," and even "madness" (DS 2730). Freedom of opinion and expression was qualified as a "most pestilential error" (DS 2731).

Montalembert summed up this attitude on the part of a closed Catholicism in the following terms: "When I am the weaker I appeal for liberty, on your principle. But when I am the stronger I deny you this same liberty, on my principle."[1]

The Church was in precious little evidence during the debate and passage by the United Nations of the Universal Declaration of the Rights of Man, on December 10, 1948, in Paris. It mistrusted these secular stirrings. Only two Catholic organizations, on the fringes of officialdom, participated in the discussions: the World Organization of Catholic Women and the International Confederation of Christian Unions.[2]

Why this hesitation, of which we are so ashamed today? Because the Church was tied to the dominant secular power. The altar was lashed to the throne. And the whole modern struggle was against the privileges of the mighty, of the state, of the upper classes.

But if the presence of the Church in the definition of human rights has left something to be desired, once those rights had been proclaimed by others, the Church's role in their defense and promotion has been crucial. True, as long as it held aloof from the path trodden by the people, as long as it kept its distance from the struggles of the oppressed for liberation and human dignity, the Church continued to manifest an insensitivity to the passion of the people. It continued to disregard the plight of those whose history is the history of rights trampled underfoot. But once it began to penetrate the world of the powerless, the Church began to feel the storm of violence and aggression with which the mighty respond to the quest for human rights.

Today we can make the following observation. The more the Church becomes a church of the people, the further the Church penetrates a continent of the poor, the more it will commit itself to human rights. On the other hand, the less a church commits itself to human rights, the less a bishop speaks out in defense of violated rights, the more distant and disincarnated from the people and their social reality the attitude and pastoral approach of this church and this bishop will be. But the distance of a bishop or church from the people is in proportion to the proximity of that bishop or church to the dominant classes, and to the capitalist state these classes control. The Church universal, meanwhile, is acquiring an ever more solid grasp of the fact that its ministry includes the defense and promotion of human rights. Church reflection and practice alike have progressed to the point where the meaning of human dignity becomes concretized in reality, and the defense and promotion of rights begins where it ought to begin.

Today we understand that human rights are principally the rights of the masses. And the masses are masses of poor. The battle for human rights, then, is the battle for the rights of the poor: for the dignity of the oppressed first and foremost, and then—moving outward from these oppressed—the dignity of all women and men.

This is the only authentic stance, either in theory or in practice. Take any other and you are caught in the game of the powerful. The mighty, too, speak of human rights—in their endeavor to put a humanistic face on their barbarous practices of exploitation and the actual violation of those rights. By posing the theme of human rights in terms of the dignity of the oppressed, we espouse both the biblical view and the best elements of the humanistic tradition, which has actually developed this theme in modern times.

HUMAN RIGHTS AS THE RIGHTS OF THE IMPOVERISHED MASSES

The historical antecedents of the various declarations on human rights, whether in the North American Revolution (1776), the French Revolution (1789), or the United Nations Declaration (1948), are found in the struggle against the pretensions of power. Thus the Magna Charta (1215), considered the first formulation of the rights of humanity, was formulated to limit the absolute power of the king. It was still elitist, however, and the rights it created were simply the privileges of the noble feudal class and the clerical caste. The rest of the population, the Third Estate, continued without any rights whatever. Only in 1689, with the Bill of Rights, were rights attributed to all citizens of the state.

Europe's perpetual slumber where the question of human rights was concerned was rudely disturbed by the sixteenth-century debates on the rights of the poor—that is, of the Indians and blacks—with the conquest of Latin America. The debates between Ginés de Sepúlveda and Bartolomé de las Casas on the nature of the Indian—in the Valladolid Disputations of 1550—stand as a landmark in this area.

Sepúlveda argued along these lines:

The fact of having cities and some sort of rational manner of life and some kind of commerce is something brought about by natural necessity, and it only serves to prove that they are not bears or monkeys, and that they are not totally lacking in reason.[3]

Similarly, Gonzalo Fernández de Oviedo (1478–1557) wrote in his *Historia General y Natural de las Indias:*

These people of the Indies, though they are rational and descended from the same stock that came out of Noah's sacred ark, have become *irrational* and *bestial* by reason of their idolatries, sacrifices and infernal ceremonies.[4]

As we see, anyone different, anyone poor and lowly, is immediately the object of contemptuous discrimination.

The question posed by Bartolomé de las Casas is the following: Have the Indians equal rights with the Spanish and the Portuguese or have they not? And his answer, like that of Vieira and other contemporary defenders of human rights, was: Yes, they have rights, and equal rights, because they are human beings. And because they are human beings, they are our neighbor. And being our neighbor they are called to the same community of the people of God, the same family of God as you and I. No inequalities or differences in religion or morality, not even the human sacrifices of the Aztecs, may be invoked as a pretext to subjugate them or violate their human rights. Such inequality in their theories or practices furnishes no grounds for dealing with them as if they were animals, or for pretending to secure their good by violent means, such as enslavement.

We know of the long disquisitions of Francisco de Vitória in Salamanca and Hugo Grotius in northern Europe in defense of the existence of the Indian soul and its inviolability in virtue of the sacredness of human nature. But all such considerations remained on the level of theoretical discussion. In practice the potentates and *encomendeiros* simply forged ahead in their thirst for conquest and greed for gold and land. No theoretical consideration mattered. Small wonder, then, that between 1532 and 1568 the total population of Mexico fell from 16,874,409 to 2,649,673. Nor were the victims brought down only by the diseases of the whites. The principal cause of the extermination was the violence and destruction wrought on their civilizations by the gangsters we call the conquistadors.[5]

The most important thing, however, is that once it became a question in the sixteenth century, the theme of human rights has never failed to occupy and preoccupy human awareness. To our very day the cry of the oppressed gives the consciences of states and societies an uneasy rest. And whenever the matter of rights rears its head, it is always from within a struggle waged by the weak against the superiority of the mighty. The Declaration of the Rights of Man at the time of the French Revolution, for example, was a protest, in the name of the emancipation of the individual, against a totalitarian state. These "inalienable and sacred natural rights" were proclaimed on foundations of equality and universality of the human being.

Despite this universality of declared intention, however, it is only too easy to perceive the social place of the proclaimers of such rights. And the proclaimers will be the beneficiaries. They will be the bourgeois, and will be the historical agents of the great liberal project that flourishes under the sign of the value of the individual, private property, and the citizen's liberty. But liberty, private property, equality, and security are not made to rest on the reciprocal relationships of human beings, on social responsibility. The rights are based on the individual's character as an individual, as a personal being separated and isolated. No wonder, then, that an elite alone benefited from the North American Bill of Rights of 1789. As a North American you had rights indeed, provided you had nothing black, Catholic, Jewish, or atheistic about you.

This was a departure from the Christian matrix of the sixteenth century, in which the rights of the Indians and blacks were defined in terms of their right to participation, their recognition as members of society *pleno jure.* A great part of the struggle for human rights today still betrays its liberal and individualistic roots. The rights at issue tend to be the rights that correspond to the interests of the bourgeois classes, such as freedom of expression, religious freedom, freedom of the press, and the right to private property.

Surely these are precious rights. Just as surely, however, they are rights exercised mainly by the mighty. The popular masses continue to live under conditions of harshest repression, and win new guarantees only when they can wrest them from their superiors by force.

Human rights, especially the right to private property, are not without limits. They may not be maintained through oppression of the poor and weak. The individual cannot be adequately considered in isolation from society as a whole. The rights of the individual cannot be defined against the rights of society. Individual rights must be harmonized with social rights. It is here that the rights of the masses in Latin America gains relevancy.

Today the rhetoric of human rights has been "hijacked," by and large, by the agencies most guilty of violating those rights: the arbitrary power systems. This is why Latin America, not without the influence of the churches, is developing an alternative language, one that will not fall victim to the ideological usage to which the theme of "human rights" is presently subjected. In Latin America the terminology that is more and more preferred is *the rights of the impoverished masses.*

The common good is principally the good of the majority. It is the product of an option for the great violated, oppressed masses. In theory and practice, democracy must begin with the marginalized. When you start with the poor, you realize how urgent it is to prioritize human rights: the right to life and the means thereto—physical integrity, health, housing, employment, social security, education—must come first. Other rights, less urgent than these, will be human rights indeed, but they will be defined from a point of departure in these even more basic rights. And here we have the concrete evidence that human rights actually coincide with a limitation on the privileges of the powerful. In order to safeguard the rights of the weakest, in order that all together may be able to create and enjoy a life of justice and communion, some limitations must be placed on the rights of the mighty.

At the close of the Third General Assembly of the Synod of Bishops, at which the assembled fathers considered the question of evangelization, they published a statement on human rights and reconciliation.[6] Their pronouncement includes an official prioritization of certain human rights on grounds of their being more basic and more threatened than others. First come the right to life and the right to nourishment. Next come socioeconomic rights on an international level, for it is here that peoples violate distributive justice. Then come political and cultural rights, by virtue of which all ought to enjoy a share in the determination of the collective lot. Finally, the Synod speaks of the right to religious liberty, that special expression of the dignity of the human person, who is capable of a free relationship with the Transcendent.

COMMITMENT OF THE CHURCHES TO HUMAN RIGHTS, ESPECIALLY THE RIGHTS OF THE POOR

Let us attempt a rapid overview of how the poor in Latin America are demanding and exercising their basic rights. First of all, we note a rapidly rising collective consciousness with respect to their dignity, and the injury to that dignity that they are suffering. This new awareness is especially evident in the mushrooming popular organizations, in the neighborhoods, and in the communities, where the humble, effective struggle for rights is being waged. Along these lines we note the various popular movements, such as the protests against shortages and the high cost of living, or the demand for a union movement independent of the control of the Ministry of Labor, which represents only the official policies of dominant interests.

Meanwhile, the churches have provided the people with a systematic education in their basic right to life and the means to life. They have also put up a courageous defense of the people's dignity. Since the 1960s Latin America has been the scene of the proliferation of so-called national security regimes, according to whose ideology anyone publicly questioning the dominant interests of the state is labeled a subversive, and becomes the victim of government surveillance, repression, torture, or even death. Even under a less totalitarian regime the human rights theme is always held in suspicion by the security agencies of Latin America. It is an uncomfortable topic for the establishment.

The churches have decided to function as a public, authoritative forum for the airing of violations of the rights of the people. The better to promote their work of denunciation and proclamation, they have created agencies such as Chile's Vicariate for Solidarity and Brazil's Rural Ministry Commission and Native Mission Council. And everywhere we see commissions for human rights, or justice and peace, secretariats for justice and nonviolence, and other groups whose purpose is the promotion of the persons and dignity of the powerless.

The intentionality of such organizations is not the defense of the corporate rights of the Church. Their purpose is to assure the Church's service to the needy among its people—regardless of their confessional or ideological definition—be they Native Americans threatened with extermination, peasants driven from their lands, or the disappeared. In their efforts to denounce the deterioration of the living and working conditions under which the population is forced to exist, the episcopates or church organizations of practically all the Latin American countries have published documents that have burst over the heads of the complacent like bombshells: "I Have Heard the Cries of My People" (1973) by the bishops of the Brazilian Northeast, "The Churches are Shouting: Marginalization of a People" (1973) by the bishops of the West Central region, and "Oppress Not Your Brother" (1974) by the hierarchy of São Paulo are some of the more outstanding.

Engagement costs. Slander, persecution, kidnappings, and the murder of laity, religious, priests, and bishops are the price Christians must pay for their commitment. But they have paid that price in the spirit of the Beatitudes, and most generously.

At the Christian grass roots particularly in the vast network of base church communities, when the people speak of human rights they practice what they preach. They get involved in a genuine pastoral ministry of the rights of the poor. They likewise vigorously demand the rights that accrue to them in their baptism, so that we have a genuine community participation in the Word, a group liturgical creativity, community coordination by the community itself, and lay participation in the drafting and execution of diocesan and parish ministries, with the laity working together with the priests council.

THEOLOGICAL FOUNDATION OF THE RIGHTS OF THE IMPOVERISHED MASSES

I have no intention of rehearsing the classic argument enunciated in the preamble to the North American Bill of Rights: that human rights are based on human equality, which in turn rests on the oneness of the creative act of God. Nor shall I belabor the anthropological grounds that have been advanced in order to found these rights. The latter, as we know, is based on the notion that, because all human beings are transcendent by virtue of their spirit, and capable of maintaining a dialogue with the Absolute, their freedom of will endows them with the capability of either bestowing meaning on their lives or frustrating those lives—endows them with the capacity to forge an eternal destiny for themselves; and that the externalization of this freedom presupposes the exercise of basic rights. Nor, finally, shall I invoke a religious, for instance, a christological, argument that says that inasmuch as every human being is in the image and likeness of God and a brother or sister of Jesus, whose humanity belongs to God, everyone is, in some sense, touched by divinity. All such premises correctly conclude to the inviolability of the human person, thus placing limits on any powers that be, and condemning any form of domination by one individual over the other.

Instead, my concern is the establishment of the rights of the poor. This is what is meant by *human rights* in our churches. Furthermore, this is the biblical approach to human rights, and the biblical theme is an important one. The Bible never speaks of human rights. The rights spoken of in the Bible belong to the orphan, the widow, the pauper, the immigrant, and the alien. There is no sidestepping the fact that biblical rights, especially in the Prophets, the Wisdom literature, and the New Testament, are the rights of the oppressed.

In the Bible the basic, electrifying assertion is, "He who oppresses the poor blasphemes his Maker, but he who is kind to the needy glorifies him" (Prov. 14:31; cf. 17:5). Everyone has someone to defend. A woman, her spouse; a man, his children; children, their parents. The poor alone have no one to look after them. And so God has taken up their cause himself. Now it is he who "executes justice for the orphan and the widow, and befriends the alien, feeding and clothing him" (Deut. 10:18; cf. Jer. 22:16, Prov. 22:22–23). Psalm 146 is equally explicit:

> Who keeps faith forever,
>   secures justice for the oppressed,
>   gives food to the hungry.
> The LORD sets captives free;
>   the LORD gives sight to the blind.
> The LORD raises up those that were bowed down. . . .
>   The LORD loves the just.
> The LORD protects strangers;
>   the fatherless and the widow he sustains.
>
> Ps. 146:6–9

The alien should be accorded the same rights and the same treatment as an Israelite (Lev. 19:33, Exod. 12:48).

God is not only the supreme guarantor of a just order, as we are accustomed to think. His principal activity is the defense of the rights of the powerless, the persecuted, the poor. God does not side with the mighty, then, who have the law at their disposition and utilize it to their own advantage. God sides with those violated in their dignity and their justice.

It pertains to the prime task of the Messiah, the Savior of the world, to exercise this divine right on behalf of the poor. Psalm 72, referring to the Messiah, says,

> For he shall rescue the poor man when he cries out,
>   and the afflicted when he has no one to help him.

> He shall have pity for the lowly and the poor;
> the lives of the poor he shall save.
>
> Ps. 72:12–13

Jesus refers to this tradition (Luke 4:17–30), as handed down in Isaiah 61:1–3 (cf. 11:1–10), in his presentation of his messianic program in the synagogue at Nazareth (Luke 4:17–30). The Beatitudes confirm Jesus' awareness that he is the liberator of the poor, of those who weep, of those who suffer hunger, injustice, or persecution (Luke 6:20–23, 5:31–32).

God is therefore the guarantor of the fundamental rights of the poor (Exod. 22:20–22). Now, these fundamental rights, because they constitute the right to life, are sacred and inalienable. They take precedence over any other right. The right to life is an infrastructural right: upon its foundation all others will be erected.

The people of Israel developed their concept of the fundamental rights of the poor on the basis of their experience as exploited aliens in the land of Egypt. The collective memory of their own experience of poverty and oppression came to be reflected in a refrain all through the Old Testament: "So you must befriend the alien, for you were once aliens yourselves in the land of Egypt" (Deut. 10:19). "You shall not do as they do in the land of Egypt, where you once lived" (Lev. 18:3). The people of Israel had been delivered by God from their own situation of oppression: they themselves, then, in their own turn, ought to attend to the oppression suffered by other weak and helpless persons.

Job expresses a keen awareness of this solidarity:

> Had I refused justice to my manservant
> or to my maid, when they had a claim against me,
> What then should I do when God rose up;
> what could I answer when he demanded an account?
> Did not he who made me in the womb make him?
> Did not the same One fashion us before our birth?
>
> Job 31:13–15

But the ultimate foundation of the rights of the poor is in the nature of God himself. For it pertains to the very essence of God to be a living God, to be the God of life. God hears, speaks, sees, and knows. He senses the cries of his people when they beg to be set free. He laughs to scorn idols that have mouths that cannot speak, ears that cannot hear, and hands that cannot feel (Ps. 115:4–8). The people of Israel place their trust in a God who intervenes in history, a God who is not far from human beings, a God whose Reign is built on a pact with women and men—a pact on behalf of life, and a pact against whatever might threaten that life.

And because God is the God of life, he takes the part of the poor and the oppressed, whose lives are threatened. The poor are not poor because they are indolent. For the biblical mentality, especially as we see it in the prophets, the poor are poor because they have been impoverished, because they have been reduced to a condition of penury. For the Bible, life is historical. No one's life is simply fated to be miserable. Regardless of their moral condition—even if they are not religious, even if they are not in his grace, and so on—God sides with the poor (cf. Puebla Final Document, no. 1142). Simply because he is the God of life, God always enters the picture when life is threatened, or when human beings deny one another life.

Let us see why this is so.

God's partiality toward the poor is not simply the product of his free will. It is a reflection of his very essence. To affirm God's predilection for the poor is simply to acknowledge a concrete reflection of the fact that, by his very essence, God is a God of life.[7]

As God is by his very nature the God of life, so it is by his very nature that he generates life. And so he succors and defends those whose lives are threatened, or who share less in the gift of life. This is why God is, in a special way, the God of the poor. The rights of the poor are rights that regard life itself, rights calculated to maintain and expand life. Therefore the rights of the poor are rights of God.

To believe in God is to believe in the life of all, especially the poor. Belief in God is incompatible with acquiescence in the death of the poor. Belief in God is irreconcilable with a sublimation of the miseries of the poor by way of an appeal to the cross or a future life. Where life is oppressed, God is oppressed. Where Christianity does not expand life, animate life, where the practices of Christians and their hierarchs fail to create space for life and the signs of life—joy, freedom, creativity—then we really must wonder what god is being preached and worshiped. For Holy Scripture it is idolatry, and not so much atheism, that is the great denial of God. The opposite of God is a false god, and the Bible is at pains to show us that wealth, power, and greed, or the amassing of wealth, are very definitely false gods, fetishes, and idols. They have their special marks, which betray them: not to speak, not to hear, not to have compassion, but to kill, to murder, to go looking for blood. And Ezekiel excoriates the idolaters:

Her nobles within her [the land] are like wolves that tear prey, shedding blood and destroying lives to get unjust gain. . . . The people of the land practice extortion and commit robbery; they afflict the poor and the needy, and oppress the resident alien without justice.

Ezek. 22:27, 29

As we see, idolaters are in the image of their gods: the idolaters too are enemies of life and procurers of the death of others. By contrast, the true God, the God of life, wills life and the Reign of freedom. If we would know where God is, we need only look where life is protected, where the poor are respected and made sharers of life.

The Scriptures propose an infallible criterion for judging whether a state or polity is in the good graces of God. We need only examine the manner in which it deals with the poor. If it marginalizes them, is contemptuous of them, if they add up to a factor of zero when the state is planning its programs, then we may be sure that we are dealing with a wicked, godless state, propelled by the whirring mechanisms of death.

It is in the New Testament that we find the strongest identification of the rights of the poor as the rights of God. First of all, it is the poor who are constituted the primary addressees of the proclamation of the Reign of God (Luke 4:18, 6:20). We shall understand the Gospel as the Good News that it is only if we understand it from a point of departure in the perspective of the poor, only if we hear it from the place of those whose lives are diminished and threatened.

Second, the Reign of God is set up in opposition to the anti-Reign. The Reign of God becomes reality only to the extent that the blind see, the lame walk, and justice is restored to the poor. Only then is there Good News: Gospel (cf. Luke 7:21–22).

Finally, the supreme criterion of salvation and perdition in the New Testament is solidarity with the last and the least. God-in-the-flesh identifies with the poor: "As often as you did it for one of my least brothers, you did it for me" (Matt. 25:40). The divine right of Jesus Christ is identical with the rights of the poor. And yet the equality of all men and women, the universality of their dignity, and the oneness of society continue to be a laughingstock. Profound historical alterations are needed if the requirements of the Reign are to be satisfied. And these necessary, profound transformations must be accomplished through attention to the pleas of the poor when they cry out for life, participation, and dignity.

EVANGELIZATION: SERVICE OF GOD AND PROMOTION AND DEFENSE OF HUMAN RIGHTS, ESPECIALLY THOSE OF THE POOR

The 1974 Synod of Bishops, in collegiality with Pope Paul VI, issued a forthright statement of the ministry of the Church on behalf of human rights, especially the rights of the lowly. "The Church," the Synod stated, "firmly believes that the promotion of human rights is an *exigency* of the Gospel, and that it must have a *central place* in its ministry." Indeed, the Synod cited a "ministry of the Church to promote human rights in the world."[8]

The bishops at Puebla clearly grasped that the struggle for human rights "may well be the original imperative of this divine hour on our continent" (Puebla Final Document, no. 320).[9] For Puebla, "human dignity is an evangelical value" (no. 1254), and an "integral part" of all evangelization (nos. 1254, 1283). The promotion and defense of human rights means primarily the promotion and defense of the "rights of the poor" (an expression used five times in the Puebla document: nos. 320, 324, 711, 1119, 1217)—which, as we have seen, are concentrated in the basic right to a human existence with a minimum of dignity.

It is the promotion and defense of the rights of the poor that satisfy the imperative of both the Old and the New Testament with regard to sacrifice and worship. Would we know what manner of sacrifice is pleasing to God? Well, then: "Learn to do good. Make justice your aim: redress the wronged, hear the orphan's plea, defend the widow" (Isa. 1:17). Jesus endorses this tradition in Mark 7:6–8: the crucial element of the law, he tells us, the thing forgotten by the Pharisees and the pious, is "justice and mercy and good faith. It is these you should have practiced" (Matt. 23:23). Evangelization, then—the bearing of the glad tidings, the bringing of the Good News—happens only when reality changes from bad to good, when the rights denied the poor are finally restored to them. Today this type of evangelization is realized only in the measure that we create conditions of solidarity with the poor, to the end that, together with the poor, we may all engage in a practice calculated to reestablish right and restore justice.

The process is fraught with conflict and tension. The poor never obtain their rights without stepping on vested pretensions and privileges. The road to liberation is strewn with these, however, and until the litter is swept aside, the resistance of the prideful will have to be accepted as a fact of life, in the spirit of the Beatitudes. The price is worth paying when the prize is liberation.

In the interim our task is to accept the mission of the Servant of Isaiah, the One who proposes to "bring forth justice to the nations. . . . A bruised reed he shall not break, and a smoldering wick he shall not quench, until he establishes justice on the earth" (Isa. 42:1, 3–4).

4. The Supernatural in the Process of Liberation

We have no systematic reflection as yet on the question, so frequently broached, of the place of the supernatural in the process of the historical liberation of the oppressed. We do note the tendency of various theological currents simply to do without the classic question of the natural versus the supernatural.[1] Some theologians even call for the deletion of the term *supernatural* from the theological lexicon. It has served its purpose in the thought of the Latin Church, we are told. Its function can now be taken over by other, less ambiguous, expressions.[2]

The *reality* of the supernatural, of course, is as crucial for Christianity as sin and grace, salvation and the Reign of God. And yet for more than fifteen centuries, Christianity expressed this reality by and large without recourse to the expression *supernatural*.[3] The word is completely absent from the New Testament. Early theologians of the stature of Origen, the Great Cappadocians, St. Augustine, St. Bernard, and St. Anselm never used the word. It appears for the first time in the sixth century, becoming common in the ninth century, to denote a reality pertaining exclusively to God as distinguished from creaturely reality. It is used synonymously with terms such as *superexcellens, supermundanus, superessentialis,* and *supersubstantialis.*[4] At the dawn of the thirteenth century, when medieval theology would reach its zenith, it was still a rare term. Only from 1256 to 1259, when St. Thomas Aquinas wrote his *Quaestiones Disputatae de Veritate,* did it have the status of a received theological category.

The word *supernatural* finally appears in the pronouncements of the papal magisterium in 1567, with the publication of the bull of Pope Pius V (1566–72) condemning the theologian Michael Baius, who had speculated in a disquieting fashion on the relationship between the human condition and divine grace (DS 1921, 1923).

THE MEANING OF THE WORD *SUPERNATURAL*

The word *supernatural* was coined to help formulate a Christian expression of the reality of the human being within the framework of Greek philosophy, which operated in terms of a category of nature.[5] We may distinguish three stages in the development of a Christian response to the status of the human being in terms of nature. The first finds its classic formulation in the great anti-Pelagian polemic of St. Augustine. Augustine moves from an examination of human nature in a perspective of God's salvific plan. Human nature appears to Augustine as decadent, the slave of sin. Through its own resources human nature will never be capable of delivering itself from this captivity, never be able to achieve its own salvation. It will be able to make wonderful strides in terms of a noble, open humanism, such as we have in the wise among the ancients. But it will be unable to lift itself up by its own bootstraps and deliver itself from sin. Not that sin has depraved the human essence. But it has deprived it—robbed it, wounded it in such a way as forever to divest it of any hope of escape from the prison of itself through efforts of its own. But God has never abandoned this human creature of his, so hopelessly turned in upon itself, but has ever hastened to its aid, opening spaces for a rehumanization that returns it, however fragilely, to the original stature of the human being. St. Augustine, and with him all of ancient theology, calls this assistance *grace,* identifying it as the gracious humanizing and divinizing presence of God himself. But Augustine understands this divine resource existentially—as part and parcel of the only concrete dispensation of God's salvation history.

A second stage in the development of a Christian conception of the supernatural occurred with the integration of Christian thought with Aristotelian philosophy in High Scholasticism. Here *nature* acquires a metaphysical denotation. Now *nature* signifies that complex of perfections or qualities that constitute a being within a determinate species. These qualities can belong to human nature constitutively, consecutively, or exigitively. Body and soul, along with the spiritual faculties, pertain to human nature constitutively. Knowledge and social institutions pertain to it consecutively—they "follow upon" human nature. The material world and human culture are the exigitive properties of human nature, inasmuch as the latter demands them for its self-realization. Now suddenly human nature is a microcosm, an island, with its own independent identity and specific end. The natural will be all that corresponds to this nature, derives from it, or is ordained to it per se. The supernatural, then, will be anything that of itself neither makes up, flows from, nor is demanded by, this nature per se, but which nevertheless is physically capable of accruing to it—and, indeed, most desirably, as it will be incomparably enriching for it. The supernatural will be anything superadded to nature by way of gift and gratuity. Hence the order of things, per se divine, the divine dispensation in humanity's regard, consisting in forgiveness of sins and a summons to an intimate, absolute communion with God, will be styled the supernatural order. The supernatural elevates nature, then, divinizing it, through a pure, free initiative on the part of God.

This approach has its validity. It exalts human reality, the potentialities of reason, and the autonomy of human activity. It has assimilated the intuitions of the Enlightenment and modernity, which had occasioned the great debates over the natural and the supernatural. The category of the supernatural was first invoked to safeguard the uniqueness of the Christian phenomenon, and of redemption as God's free gift to human reality.

On the negative side, this view is extrinsicist. Here, grace comes only from without. It has no historical pertinency to a nature closed off in its splendid identity. Is it possible to desire and long for a reality that, when all is said and done, has no original connection with us, a reality simply superadded to us from without? These are the questions that have forever dogged this compromise formulation between the natural philosophy of the ancients and the emancipation of the modern human being on the one side, and on the other the uniqueness of Christianity, which asserts the graciousness of a God who has loved us and delivered us.

The third formulation is the child of modern and postmodern thinking. Recent philosophical currents have striven to plumb still further the specificity of human nature. What ultimately makes human nature human? Kant, Hegel, and the existentialists have been the main artisans of the contemporary vision of human nature as spirit and freedom. The essence of the human being is spirit: the human being's character is one of absolute openness, transcendence, and "transdescendence." The exercise of human freedom permits men and women to construct themselves; then to transform the world, creating culture; and finally to project themselves in a relationship with the absolute of God. It is characteristic of this free spirit to be the seat of infinite, absolute desire. Only the Absolute, in bestowing itself as a free gift upon this all-desiring spirit, can assuage the latter's oceanic appetite.

In other words, nature has no center. Only through its adjustment to a center situated outside itself can it attain happiness and full self-realization. Only God concretizes the human utopia. The cry of women and men for God is nothing but the echo of the voice of God himself calling them to communion with him, and in that communion to absolute self-actualization. In this conceptualization the supernatural acquires a genuine affinity with the natural. No longer is the latter understood as self-contained in a specific identity and finality. Now the natural itself is grasped in its interior transcendent dynamism, a thrust surpassing any historical concretization and remaining permanently open—that is, coming to rest only in the reality known as God.[6]

This philosophical reflection has been complemented with a specifically christological one. Christ is the one human being with a capacity for receiving God totally. Christ is the *homo* of the *Ecce Homo;* the paragon of humanity, with a capacity for God himself; the archetype of every human being. We are all created to the image and likeness of Christ. We are all of us sons and daughters in the eternal Son. Accordingly, we too enjoy a capacity for an infinite relationship with God, an unrestricted reception of the divinity within us. The *ratio* of human nature resides in its capacity for the impetration of that total self-communication of God that found its perfect historical realization in Jesus of Nazareth. Pure human nature, a human nature closed in upon itself, does not exist in the concrete. Historical human nature is always exposed to, open to, the reception of the eternal Son. The only order willed by God, the only divine dispensation, is the supernatural order and dispensation. There is no such thing, concretely, as a merely intrahistorical, anthropological finalization. There is no two ends of the human being, one natural and the other supernatural, the latter being superadded by way of complement to the former. There exists only and solely the supernatural end, in respect of which women and men either realize themselves or ontologically collapse.

Then is it still meaningful to speak of the natural at all? Yes, in the sense of creatureliness. The human being is creature, a being created to the image and likeness of the Creator (Gen. 1:27). As such—by nature, then—it is distinct from God. But it was never created with any other finality than to stand in a relationship with God. When it accepts that finality, accepts God and the project of God that makes itself present in the mediations of justice, solidarity, forgiveness, and a communion of sisters and brothers, then it is in a condition of grace. When it rejects God, and fixates on its own project—that of centering upon itself, domination of others, and the violent frustration of nature—then it is in a condition of sin. The "purely natural" is the fact of human creation, the fact of the existence of a human person who is spirit and freedom, capable either of humbly receiving God or of pridefully rejecting him. The specificity, the distinction of the human being, is its concrete capability of union with God, its concrete capability of a reconciliation with God to the extent that God becomes incarnate, thus communicating himself absolutely. Over and above this natural, creational aspect of itself, however, human nature finds itself ever called by God, ever under the sign of the rainbow, ever the object of a divine offer of dialogue and communion, to which, unhappily, human beings can always deny themselves, and historically have denied themselves.

HISTORY AND HEARTS STEEPED IN GRACE

As a result of our considerations, you now have a better grasp of the fact that the purpose of the coinage and use of the term *supernatural* was to enable the Christian vision of human existence to express itself in a nonbiblical, Greek world. The concept has now fulfilled its historical function, and the terminology itself can be abandoned. The reality signified by the term, of course, continues to be utterly relevant: in our day, however, this reality can be translated with less ambiguity by means of expressions such as *transcendence* or *infinite openness.* Today the reality of the supernatural is more relevantly conceptualized as a projection toward the Absolute. It was not without reason that the celebrated document of the Second Vatican Council, *Gaudium et Spes,* simply abandoned the concept of the supernatural as the theoretical instrument for expressing human activity in the world under the action of God's grace. The Council no longer speaks of the human being's natural and supernatural calling, but of its *integral vocation,* its calling to integrate heaven and Earth, the exigencies of history with the imperatives of transcendence (cf. *Gaudium et Spes,* nos. 10, 11, 57, 59, 61, 63, 91; *Ad Gentes,* no. 8). And a well-known Roman theologian comments:

Such a reserve [on the part of the Council, as expressed in *Gaudium et Spes*], certainly intentional, reflects a tendency in contemporary theology. The disadvantages inherent in the use of the concept of the "supernatural" are well known, and various attempts are currently under way to explain the gift of Christ in such a way as simultaneously to safeguard both its transcendence with respect to the creature—its "supernatural" character—and its positive aspect in its relation to the totality of the Christian message.[7]

If it is true that human existence is characterized by the constant summons to transcendency—if human beings order themselves, positively or negatively, to God or the Reign of God (God's project) in all that they do, think, and say—then we must also posit the unity of history. History is always the history of salvation or perdition, the history of human beings and God in dialogue, in breach, in redemption and liberation.

All human practices, even those maintained outside the Christian space, or without any religious reference, even atheistic practices, occur within the dimension of grace/sin. Hence the theological value of human beings' whole historical reality, their culture, and their various modes of production. All historical articulations contain an objective theological reality, even if we do not wish it, even if our consciousness has not risen to an awareness of it. This ontic reality can be "conscientized"—represented in a religious discourse, indeed in a theological reflection. Grace steeps human history and permeates the human heart. So does sin. Concretely, human history is organized in a difficult dialectic of sin and grace, obedience and rebellion, both the realization and the frustration of God's plan in history existing side by side. Augustine, in a formulation whose secret he, if anyone, had experienced to the hilt, could actually say, in all realism, "Omnis homo Christus, omnis homo Adam": Each of us is at once Christ and Adam, the new human being and the old, heaven and hell.

One of the purposes of an appeal to the theme of the supernatural in a Christian theology of the Greek variety was to safeguard the preeminence of God's initiative. The great, prime reality is the supernatural. The natural is but the antechamber and infrastructure of a plan and design whose protagonist is principally God. God has willed to associate to his life other lives, and to his love new companions who also love. History is human because it is done by creatures. But these creatures have been created by God's love, and human history yearns for, and obtains, a divine history. God enters into communion with human beings. Jesus Christ is the crossroads of these two paths, and the history we read in him has as its ultimate subject the very Son of God.

THE SUPERNATURAL AND CRITICAL ALIENATION IN THE NAME OF A LIBERATIVE FAITH

Christianity runs a serious risk of alienation and ideologization when it regards the supernatural as something extrahistorical, as a reality adventitious to the natural, as a kind of "second floor" of the human edifice, as something deprived of any affinity with the reality of the human being. We hear that Christianity has to do with the supernatural, not with the natural. Christian activity must be inserted into the supernatural, and the supernatural is communicated by the institutions of the sacred: sacraments; celebration; meditation on, and assimilation of, the biblical revelation; acts of faith, hope, love; and all the other virtues practiced within the body of the Church. Theology must deal with the supernatural. It should leave the natural to the profane sciences. Merely natural reason is exercised in the domain of the natural, whereas reason enlightened by faith or bathed in the supernatural concerns itself with supernatural realities.

This understanding has generated a Christianity disengaged from history, a Christianity absent from the great historico-social events that have shaken the past three hundred years of humanity's pilgrimage on this planet. Inasmuch as the supernatural, in this acceptation, is *per se* beyond the pale of experience—only the natural can be the object of experience—access to it is had only through a faith acceptance of truth, and through the teaching of the magisterium. This understanding of Christianity brings it very near, if indeed it does not identify it with, ideology. The truth of Christianity is exempt from verification, as it is of its very nature beyond inquiry. After all, being supernatural, in this interpretation, it will transcend any rational or historical criterion of verification.

Here Christianity runs the risk of being fetishized. It obliges itself to believe in a supernatural order in the form of a world totally apart from the one in which we live, accessible only to verbal, intellectual faith, communicated only by propositions of faith held as supernatural revelation. The historical character of these propositions is of no account. How they have arisen, how they have been developed by the faith community or by the sacred authors, who, in their own turn, have lived an experience of God and grace, and have expressed that experience in a historically determinate language, does not come into the picture.

The great insufficiency of this extrinsicist comprehension of the supernatural resides in its exclusion of an insertion of the natural into Christianity's reflections and concerns. But it is in the natural order that we have our dramas and conflicts, that human beings confront one another in the fierce struggles of class with class, in processes of liberation, and in the transformation of the world. But all of this seems irrelevant for Christians. After all, it remains inscribed in the natural order. Even a version of the supernatural as an expression of the human being's infinite openness has frequently failed to emerge from a pure philosophical formalism. We have failed to translate *supernatural existential* in terms of human beings' concrete lives, struggles, and insertion into a conflictive history. The most the supernatural has been able to attain has been a personalistic approach in terms of a theology of encounter, dialogue, and communion as loci of a verification of transcendence. The social and historical realities that dominate today's awareness have been all but ignored in our theological considerations of the supernatural.

As Christians we know that human history is stepped in grace and that the human heart is permeated with grace. This fact is guaranteed, then. This is our premise. It is not the task of theology, once this datum of revelation has been assimilated, to bog down in a series of pure tautologies. Theology must draw conclusions. The questions to be examined in the light of this premise must be relevant ones. Theological discourse must not consist simply in a long series of restatements of the issue of whether nature is called to an ultimate destiny within the mystery of God. The relevant questions to be examined in the light of this premise bear on those historical articulations that demonstrate the force and validity of the supernatural as the realization of the plan of God, and on those articulations that thwart that plan and construct the project of flesh and sin.

A concern with these questions would lead the theologian to a realization that the crucial antithesis is not the natural versus the supernatural, but the supernatural order of grace versus the supernatural order of sin. Then the next step would be the historicization of grace and sin in terms of the reality that afflicts us. Where, in our reality, does sin cluster and abound? Where, in our reality, is grace embodied? Then we would perceive that the great questions posed to Christian awareness and today's theological meditation are the questions of oppression and liberation, in religion and in society—the questions of the nonperson and the person, the underworld and the world, underdevelopment and development.[8] These are the great questions that challenge us today. And their challenge is not so much that of constructing a better interpretation of human beings and their history, but of transforming society in the direction of participation and a communion of sisters and brothers.

With these questions we finally touch on the issue before us: the supernatural and the process of liberation. I trust that the reasons for my recasting of the issue are clear. The questions translate into the following terms: To what extent is the process of the liberation of the poor ordered to the Reign of God? And how is human liberation a vehicle and a part of grace and salvation?

THEOLOGICAL RELEVANCE OF THE STRUGGLE OF THE OPPRESSED FOR LIBERATION

The theology of liberation springs from the deepest heart of a commitment and practice whose finality is the liberation of the oppressed. It is not a matter of placing one more question—liberation—on the crowded theological agenda. It is a matter of thinking the totality of the content of the faith and the Gospel from a point of departure in a practice of liberation and an option for the poor against their poverty. This is the authentic nature of the theology of liberation.

Ever since the 1960s all Latin America has been the scene of a remarkable popular mobilization. The oppressed are beginning to be aware of the causes of their impoverishment. Class organizations, such as unions, political parties, popular mobilizations of every order, have been of service in the attempt to transform society into one in which the interests of the entire population are considered. Today countless Christians, particularly in the working classes (as with Workers' Catholic Action) and scholastic milieus (as with Christian University Youth) have taken up the struggle. Their practice goes beyond a merely reformist perspective, which leaves the system untouched. They are aiming at a different sort of society. They have begun to reflect on Christianity's contribution to the liberation process, as well as to reflect on this process itself as a reality endowed with a dimension of grace, salvation, and the "good things of the Reign of God." It has been this ferment that lies at the basis of the complex of intuitions constituting today's so-called theology of liberation.[9]

This is not the place to rehearse the main theoretical and practical moments in the constitution of the theology of liberation, or to show its ties to the great classical Catholic theology.[10] What I propose is to briefly analyze how this new theological current sees the connection between grace and human commitment in function of liberation. In classical parlance, we shall be attempting to ascertain the relationship of the supernatural with the natural process of the struggle for liberation.

History Is One: The History of Oppression and Liberation

The theology of liberation insists that there is only one history, and that this history, whatever its other dimensions, is also the history of salvation and perdition.[11] A formulation of the antithesis between sin and grace in terms of oppression and liberation arises from the superimposition of the lens of grace/sin on the field of the social, which is the most determinative instance of our perception of reality today. Now, if theology means to be able to identify the presence of sin and grace in society, it will be obliged to undertake the most rigorous possible analysis of the mechanism and functioning of that society. The particular frame of reference for the interpretation of history and society that the theology of liberation adopts is the one it hopes will afford it the best lens for identifying instances of injustice, oppression, and a denial of participation to the people, as well as the presence of more justice, more human communion, and more political and social participation. The instrumental mediation adopted by the theology of liberation for this analysis, with the intent of thereupon subjecting the results of this antecedent analysis to the illumination of a faith perspective in order to render a theological judgment on the reality under consideration, has been the dialectical approach developed by the revolutionary critical tradition. But liberation theology has adopted neither the gamut of philosophical implications historically connected with this particular critical analysis of reality (those of dialectical materialism), nor its strategic implications (those of a class struggle)—as represented, for example, in historical Marxism. By no means does the theology of liberation become the slave of its analytical tool. The latter is utilized only to the extent that it can help provide a more lucid understanding of the mechanisms that generate impoverishment and a clearer vision of possible alternatives to a capitalist society.

This analytical mediation, or another, equally effective one, were another to present itself, is basic and indispensable to a theology of the social, economic, and political aspects of human reality. Without it, that theology would fall victim either to a naive empiricism, or to a functionalism capable of legitimating the prevailing order of oppression of the poor, who constitute the vast majority of our people. Thus this theology would fail in its proper mission of the denunciation of injustice and the proclamation of communion. (Puebla is completely aware of the need for this antecedent analysis.) Without it, evangelization will fail:

The Church has been acquiring an increasingly clear and deep realization that evangelization is its fundamental mission; and that it cannot possibly carry out this mission without an ongoing effort to know the real situation and to adapt the gospel message to today's human beings in a dynamic, attractive, and convincing way. [Puebla Final Document, no. 85][12]

Were it to dispense with an antecedent analysis of reality, the Church would risk deciphering as grace and liberation what is nothing of the kind, as, for example, mere assistance or paternalism. By the same token, it would risk misinterpreting as sin and oppression what is not necessarily sin and oppression at all, such as the organization of the poor, a preferential option for the poor, or indeed the actual critical, dialectical reading of social reality itself.[13]

SECULAR VERSION OF THE PRESENCE OF THE REIGN OF GOD

This unitary, dialectical perspective on history, in which all history is seen as sin or grace or both, oppression or liberation or both, enables us to distinguish the presence of the Reign of God and its blessings in realities that do not call themselves the Reign of God or divine. All secular activity, such as political activity, the struggle of the oppressed, a commitment to the poor on the part of their allies (on the part of organic intellectuals or a cross-section of other classes, for instance), can be the vehicle of God's cause in the world, the vessel of the Reign of God and the generator of the blessings of that Reign (justice, the eradication of discrimination, more effective and equitable forms of popular participation, and the like).

But if we would know whether a given practice is indeed a vehicle of the Reign, we must attend to more than simply whether that practice so styles itself. The only valid criterion for making the appraisal in question is objective goodness. In other words, what really matters are ethical criteria. To what extent does such and such a practice generate social benefits for all and not just for a social elite? How does such and such a policy go about attending to the demands of justice? How does this or that particular state attempt to meet the vital interests of its entire population, especially the interests bound up with life itself—food, employment, health, education, housing? The Reign comes by way of mediations that define their hierarchy of priorities in function of the collective interest, rather than in terms of advantages to particular segments of society, such as the economically or academically privileged.

And so, we see, reality deemed profane has objectively either a divine or an antidivine dimension—a supernatural dimension, then. All reality, to the eyes of faith, has its connections with God, and has them independent of our subjectivity. It is the task of the person of faith to discern this materially theological dimension and the task of the theologian to formalize it in an adequate language. The objectively theological character of presence or absence of God in reality is thus transformed into a subjectively theological reality as well, through an explicit, conscious theological discourse upon that reality.

RELIGIOUS VERSION OF THE PRESENCE OF THE REIGN OF GOD

The Christian community, in all of the various local churches, becomes aware of the presence of God in history. It then gathers in the name of this faith to celebrate the deeds of God in the accomplishments of women and men, and to commit itself—for even more reasons now than the perfectly valid profane ones—to the inauguration of the blessings of the Reign of God in the world, particularly in the milieu of the poor. In this wise it renders its own version, creates its own interpretation, of the Reign of God in the historical present.

The Christian community is the vehicle of a type of discourse called the religious. Through this discourse real liberation—liberation that objectively expands the space of freedom for all men and women, starting with the oppressed—is seen as the presence of grace. Now, human beings are not the only authors of this process. The principal Author is God himself. And so the human agents of this deliverance refuse to permit its Divine Cause to abide in anonymity, but profess, worship, and proclaim him. The community celebrates the mighty works of God in the liturgy, elaborates its own proper discourse upon liberation and the whole dimension

of salvation—its catechetical, pastoral, and theological discourse—
and charts human beings' and society's Christian utopia, along
with the practical mediations, or ethos, of the concretization of
that utopia in history.

Of course, the mere fact of its awareness of salvation and consequent access to a theological discourse by no means guarantees
that the Christian community actually liberates, actually becomes
a positive mediation of God's grace. It must also make a corre-
sponding commitment. It must enter upon a practice marked by
solidarity with the poor. Only thus will this community actualize
salvation. Only thus will its sacramental function acquire meaning
and authenticity.

The first, primary element in the rationale of Christian community is its function as the vehicle of liberation. Of course, all
women and men are under the obligation of being bearers of
liberation. What is specific to the Christian community is only its
capacity to signalize this reality, render it conscious, proclaim it to
all—and thereby bring it about that more persons not only take
account of this reality, but render it explicit for themselves in an
act of attachment to God by faith, thereby incorporating themselves into the body of those who so signalize this liberative practice that they also perform.

EVANGELIZING MISSION OF THE CHURCH

Here we touch on a crucial matter. What is the Church's mission? To be sure, it will be inscribed within the religious field. But
it will scarcely be reducible to that field. To labor under this
misapprehension would be to fall victim once more to the dualism
we had overcome, whereby natural and supernatural, sacred and
profane, worldly and divine, would be materially distinct realities.
The apostolic exhortation *Evangelii Nuntiandi* (1975) broaches the
issue directly, emphasizing the urgency of transcending a double
dualism, one in the area of the political, the other in the area of
the religious. Paul VI denies that the Church may legitimately
"reduce her mission to the dimensions of a simply temporal project" (*Evangelii Nuntiandi,* no. 32).[14] But neither will it brook a reduc-

tion of that mission to the domain of the religious: "The Church is certainly not willing to restrict her mission only to the religious field and dissociate herself from man's temporal problems" (no. 34). The mission of the Church retains the same dimensions as those of the mission of its founder, Jesus Christ. It evangelizes all dimensions of human existence, then: the interior dimension, as when it strives to humanize our passions; the interpersonal dimension, as when it assists us in overcoming the spirit of vengeance, forgiving our enemies and striking a relationship of communion with our brothers and sisters; and the social dimension, as in our commitment to those oppressed by hunger and the violation of their rights (cf. Matt. 25:36–41), and the upbuilding of just relationships among all. Thus this mission is accomplished in the profane as well as in the religious area. Indeed, no dimension of life, individual or social, falls outside its scope. The field of endeavor of the evangelical, evangelizing mission of the Church is life itself, life in its whole length, breadth, and depth. In other words, it is the vocation of the Church both to see to it that there are Christian communities living the spirit of the Gospel—hence the crucial importance of ecclesial reality as such—and to see to it that society enjoy the reinforcement of mechanisms calculated to generate social justice, popular participation in society, and structural transformations of that society in the direction of more democratic forms of social intercourse. In either area, in the profane or in the sacred, albeit under distinct signs, the Reign of God and its blessings become reality.

THE RELATIONSHIP BETWEEN CHRIST'S SALVATION AND HUMAN LIBERATION

If grace, then—the supernatural—is genuinely mediated wherever we have true liberation, what specific relationship can we establish between the salvation brought by Jesus Christ and the liberation process?

Paul VI, in the apostolic exhortation just cited, teaches

The Church links human liberation and salvation in Jesus Christ, but she never identifies them, because she knows through revelation, historical experience and the reflection of faith that not every notion of liberation is necessarily consistent and compatible with an evangelical vision of man, things, and events. [*Evangelii Nuntiandi*, no. 35]

Let us notice, however, that the pope speaks not of processes of liberation, but of notions of liberation. Any process of liberation worthy of the name, any process of liberation that actually liberates, will necessarily actualize the salvation of Jesus Christ. It indeed happens that understandings of liberation that are actually misunderstandings perpetuate oppression or only change the cast, leaving the drama, the oppressive practices and structures, intact. But with respect to concrete reality, we can say that where there is genuine liberation—liberation in conformity with ethical criteria—there salvation is communicated.

But what is the precise relationship between salvation and liberation?

By salvation we understand the human and cosmic situation totally liberated from all threat to life and fully realizing God's plan for creation. Accordingly, the concept of salvation includes the eschatological, transhistorical, ultimate moment of reality. Thus Paul VI can speak of "a transcendent and eschatological salvation, which indeed has its beginning in this life but which is fulfilled in eternity" alone (*Evangelii Nuntiandi*, no. 27). And yet: "The Church strives always to insert the Christian struggle for liberation into the universal plan of salvation which she herself proclaims" (no. 38; cf. no. 9). There is no identification, then, between (eschatological) salvation and (historical) liberation. Definitive salvation is surely anticipated, concretized, and historicized in authentic liberations, but it is not exhausted there. Definitive liberation is open to a fullness not yet attained in history, and indeed impossible of attainment in the framework of history.

On the other hand, historical liberations are not only historical. They are sacraments of a salvation—that is, of a full liberation still in process and present as promise—definitively present in the life, death, and Resurrection of Jesus Christ. Salvation is not identifiable *with* historical liberations, because the latter are always phenomena of the framework of history, and so are fragmentary, never full. But salvation is identifiable *in* historical liberations introduced by human beings. That is, salvation is concretized, manifested, and anticipated in these historical liberations. Accordingly, salvation and liberation do not coincide. Salvation and (historical) liberation are (inadequately) distinct.[15] Salvation constitutes a larger reality and concept, although it includes, contains within itself—both as reality and as concept—all genuine historical liberations. The latter, for their part, open out upon liberations that are ever more integral, in an asymptotic approach to the point of that supreme, eschatological expression of liberation which is the perfect liberty of the daughters and sons of God, the just of all nations, races, and tongues who have received the gift of God in history.

From this perspective it is less difficult to grasp that human activity is never merely human, never merely immanent, never merely natural. Human activity is always penetrated, sustained, animated, adopted, and sublimated by the divine activity.

In parallel fashion the divine activity in history is never only divine. It utilizes created mediations, both human—individual and social—and cosmic, in order to become incarnate, in order to become present and realized.

This reciprocal relationship between the uncreated and created activities has its paradigm—but its mysteric character, too—in the mystery of the Incarnation. There are not two liberations, any more than there are two "Jesuses," two persons. In the soteriological case, as in the christological, there is but one mystery, in two dimensions: in the language of the christological metaphysics of the Council of Chalcedon, two natures, one human, the other divine, in an encounter without confusion, without alteration, without division, and without separation (DS 293, 302, 509, 555).

AN ETHOS FOR THE NEW CHRISTIAN: UNIVERSAL OPENNESS, ROOTED IN THE IDENTITY OF FAITH

Christians who have assimilated the notion that salvation is actually under way in history, and that in the area of the social it is concretized in historical liberations, adopt a new practice. No longer is their Christianity a purely religious practice—a matter of going to church, receiving the sacraments, and practicing such and such private, family, or liturgical devotions. Nor, on the other hand, has it suddenly become a matter of merely profane practice, such as assisting the poor, or some other political activity performed simply and exclusively for its own sake. Now Christianity is embodied in a social practice—a practice born of meditation on the Word of God, and taking its inspiration in the activity of God coupled with that of human beings. As a social activity this new Christian practice is necessarily born in the world of the profane. But its placenta is the Gospel. Thus it is textured in sacred space and secular. The encounter with God leads us toward an encounter with the human being, especially in the poor. And the encounter with others enriches the encounter with God. Scripture sheds light on life, and life sheds light on Scripture.

Here, then, we have the synthetic vision that enables Christians to live in the presence of God at every moment, whether at prayer in their communities or in action in their groups. God acts in both places. A new spirituality emerges: a spirituality of simultaneous involvement and celebration. Suddenly the materiality of existence is the occasion for thanksgiving, petition, and praise. Here is an integrated spirituality, a wholeness that enables Christians to form deep, serious ties even with women and men who are not Christians, yet who are on fire with the same desires, who go in quest of the same liberation. Christians see these others, too, as builders of the Reign. They see the presence of God at work in them. This new kind of Christian lives a commitment to a struggle without falling victim to the spirit of violence. Now Christians transform the Gospel imperatives into a social behavior that humanizes, that transforms reality.

We need only read some of the many hundreds of reports published by the base communities in their bulletins. These documents record the actual practice of these "new Christians." They fairly teem with concrete examples of the interpenetration of the evangelical (the supernatural) with the social (the natural). Here are Christians who strive for concrete, historical liberations, but liberations born of faith. What better way to illustrate this new ethos, which our communities have assimilated, than to transcribe portions of some of these reports? Their meaningfulness is striking, both in the practice, and in the theory behind the practice. The extracts that I shall cite are from the report of a regional assembly of base church communities held in Vitória, ES, December 20, 1977.[16]

POLITICAL DIMENSION OF FAITH

The word *política* in Portuguese has two meanings. It means "policy," and it means "politics." We use it when speaking of a "sage policy," a "policy on education," a "coffee policy," a "policy for the Rio Doce Valley," a "policy for Cobraice." A policy is any conscious, organized approach to a problem. We have policies for the affairs of our everyday lives. They help us organize our behavior and attain our ends.

In its other meaning, *política* is the art of working for the community, for the good of all. Thus it means "politics," in the original sense of that word, that is, "the organized seeking of the common good."

Our communities see politics, then, as a set of policies drawn up and carried out for the common good:

When we go to the root of all of these problems of oppression and injustice, we find that what has gone wrong is the overall system of societal organization. In other words, we find the "sin of the world," the collective sin of all humanity.

But societal organization is dependent upon politics (or "policy"). Policy, politics, is present everywhere. It envelops our whole life.

Christ came to teach us what the "common good" really is. His preaching was policy, then, and politics, in the best sense, the original sense. In fact, he centered his teaching on a politics: that of the Reign of God.

If people hope to have a better society, a new world, they shall have to do more than simply keep up a line of patter about "living as brothers and sisters and building a world of communion." We are going to have to struggle. We are going to have to exert some effort if we hope to change society's distorted organization. This is the only way in which we shall "take away the sin of the world." And the only means will be political activity. The change will come from the bottom up. It is the little ones who are going to effectuate it. The great and mighty have no wish for change. In fact, they come right out and say, "God willing, things will go on as they are." But the weak, the little ones, say, "God willing, this is all going to change." This will come about, however, only if these same little ones exert pressure from below. It has been ever thus, all through the history of humanity.

Christians who say, "I don't want anything to do with politics" are only fooling themselves. They may as well be saying, "Who cares if the world goes to the devil? It's not up to me to help Christ 'take away the sin of the world.'" When we say we "don't want anything to do with politics," or that "the Church shouldn't meddle in politics"—that's politics! This attitude simply supports the distorted politics that stalks our land and creates such inequality and inequity.

There are a number of widespread misconceptions behind the notion that "the Church should keep out of politics":

1. Faith and life should be kept separate.
2. Politics is necessarily dirty, self-seeking.
3. Politics divides families and communities.
4. "You can't beat city hall." Politicians will always manage to keep us in the dark about what is really going on, so that they can run things their way.
5. Politics is just a game, like soccer.

The Church should raise the political consciousness of the people—help the people open their eyes, participate in decisions, and thus improve their government.

As for party politics: a political party should group together people with more or less the same ideas about what is good for the people and how they should be governed. These ideas are expressed in what we call a party platform.

A genuinely democratic country must have more than one political party. Then each individual can choose the party that best represents his or her way of thinking, as long as the party actually seeks the common good. Therefore church authorities should not support any particular party if there is more than one party working for the welfare of the people. Christians should have the freedom to choose their party and their candidates—consciously and responsibly, of course. Only in particular instances should church authorities say, "The only right way to vote is to vote for such and such a party." They must say this only when some particular party is the only one with a platform that reflects the genuine common good.

THEOLOGICAL ELEMENTS IN THE COMMUNITY REPORTS

(There were also theological investigations carried out at the Vitória meeting, and a great many of the statements in the reports reflect this. Here are a few of them.)

1. All men and women are the sons and daughters of God. Therefore they are all brothers and sisters, and equal to one another.
2. Unhappily, however, there is the fact of sin, with its terrible consequences. The world fails to follow its Father's plan, and so must suffer a great deal of misery, and many social inequities.
3. This is a challenge to the mission of the Church. That mission is to preach the Gospel, give direction to the faithful, "proclaim and denounce," and battle injustice and evil wherever they are found.
4. But the Church can meet this challenge adequately only if its testimony is genuine. And its testimony will be genuine only if it consists of more than words—only if it testifies also, and mainly in deeds, in work for the common good.
5. Faith calls for works, and the actions and labors of our communities are always based on, and inspired in, faith.
6. Each member of the community is called to a task within that community, in accordance with his or her particular gifts and qualities. Thus all must toil for the good of all. This is St. Paul's doctrine of the Body of Christ.
7. We are all made in the image and likeness of God. Therefore each of us is very precious. Our communities are constantly discovering new concrete value in the human person, and are making a special effort to help the poor discover their personal value.

8. As the communities journey down the path to liberation, the Way and the Model, the Center of all, is Christ.

9. And Christ's great commandment and teaching is effective, actual love for all of our brothers and sisters. All of our communities keep this mighty truth constantly before their eyes.

(Speaking more "ecclesially":)

10. People see in our communities a powerful and important sacramental renewal. No longer are the sacraments like empty ritual. Now they express a most serious commitment. Hence a thorough preparationand"consciousness-raising"isnecessarybeforereceivingthem.

11. As a result of this more thoroughgoing preparation, our liturgies also become more vibrant and meaningful, and benefit from more community participation.

12. Even in our celebrations, then, faith and life draw ever nearer one another. No longer is our religion "the opium of the people."

13. And so a great Christian commitment emerges—the commitment to help build a new world, the commitment to struggle for justice and equality for everyone.

14. [Strongly suggested in the reports, but only implicitly:] A diversification of church ministries appears, and the creation of numerous lay ministries.

15. [Likewise only implicit:] Another ecclesial element enhanced by this new union between faith and life is ecclesial communion, in the organic relationship between our base groups and their particular churches [their dioceses] and the Church universal.

16. [Only implicit, but again a strong element, are the positive and negative aspects of so-called popular piety.]

WHAT GOD DO WE WORSHIP?

The basic question, for us and for all Christians, is, What God do we acknowledge? Here is the summary that went up on the chalkboard:

1. We all suffer from the grave temptation to invent gods. Hence the importance of the question What God do we acknowledge?

2. Acceptance of the Christian God entails:

An acknowledgment in practice that every man and woman is the image of God

The construction of a community without injustice or oppression

The perception that to despise or to wrong the human person is to despise or to wrong God

The perception that the Christian response to God is lived in the reality of the ordinary everyday

The recognition that God becomes our brother and our sister, and that he elevates love-in-action to the most important thing in the Christian life

The recognition that Christ lived his voluntary impoverishment in order to enrich others

The building of a community without inequality or injustice

3. The Church is assailed by the temptation to power. Will the Church merely assist the poor, or will it be poor?

4. The twin roots of our community-building are our reality and the Word of God.

5. The sacred destiny of our pilgrimage is *liberation* in the *liberations*— plenary, eschatological Salvation, the Salvation and Liberation that is "not yet" as such, but that "already is" in the piecemeal, temporal liberations and rescues of history.

5. How Ought We to Celebrate the Eucharist in a World of Injustice?

The Eucharist is at the very heart of our faith. In the Eucharist, salvation history is compressed and condensed, and God becomes maximally present.[1] The church community feeds on the Eucharistic Body of Christ to become the Mystical Body of Christ. The Eucharist is communion with the Lord, and his everlasting sacrifice rendered visible in celebration. The Eucharist is the sacrament of a Presence that bestows Itself on human beings without interruption. The Eucharist is thanksgiving for the gift of salvation bestowed on us by the Father in Christ and the Spirit. The Eucharist is festival—the celebration in which the Church expresses its unity while creating that unity.

The mystery of the Eucharist contains all of these aspects at once, and the pedagogy of faith encourages us to regard them in their integral wholeness and experience them to the full. Still, in the ebb and flow of history, certain aspects will invariably be emphasized over others. For some Christians the eucharistic celebration is basically the performance of an act of worship and adoration of Christ's mysterious presence under the appearances of bread and wine. For others this same celebration is impetration: it asks and obtains an intimate communion with the Lord, the font of our salvation.

To emphasize certain aspects of this mystery is not necessarily to deny the others. It only means leaving others out of explicit, reflexive account, in function of this or that particular Christian way of life. In Latin America there are Christians whose entire life is one of commitment to the people's quest for liberation. Here

Christians join forces with the people in their struggle to assert their dignity, and in their defense of their land and homes. The Christians who make this commitment take their inspiration from the Word of God and communion with the Church. Naturally, then, they will emphasize aspects of the Eucharist that they find particularly meaningful in terms of their liberative engagement. These women and men ask questions such as, Is the eucharistic worship legitimate in the midst of a situation of gross institutional injustice? Does it have any meaning to celebrate the memory of Jesus when the celebrants constitute a community of oppressed and oppressors, "celebrating" side by side? In a situation of essential conflict, may we celebrate Mass—may we ritually recall Jesus' surrender, his deed of love—while permitting everything to go on as before? Is there any justification for celebrating the Eucharist at grand public events—those great, massive civil solemnities with which we are all so familiar? We shall reflect on these questions from a point of departure in Jesus' last meal with his Apostles, together with the understanding the primitive Church had of this meal.

THE LAST SUPPER: JOY IN A CONTEXT OF DEATH

Jesus' Last Supper occurs in a paradoxical context. To be sure, he finds it an occasion of joy. It is an intimate encounter with his friends. But it is a grave occasion, too, for it is a farewell meal, an occasion of profound seriousness, for Jesus is about to die.[2] The Last Supper is the prolongation and culmination of the series of special meals that Jesus has taken with others in the course of his public life. This last meal will express God's communion with human beings in his Reign (Matt. 22:1–4). By dining with sinners Jesus had sought to make it clear that the Father was inviting them to a reconciliation (Matt. 9:9–13, 11:19; Luke 19:1–10). In one of these meals he had told a sinner, "Your sins are forgiven" (Luke 7:48). Jesus' practice of making the common meal one of the focuses of his activity reflects the basic practice of his life. Where the goods of this world are concerned, Jesus invites us to practice a sharing with the poor (Mark 10:21). In human relations he asks an attitude of service (Luke 22:26: "Let the greater among you be as the junior, the leader as the servant"). His exhortations on the subject of community (Matt. 23:8: we are all sisters and brothers, daughters and sons of the same Father) and equality (John 13:14: "You must wash each other's feet") are consistent with the rest of his preaching and practice. Wherever societal values and ideals are at stake, Jesus encourages only love, forgiveness, solidarity with the marginalized, and filial openness to God.

Jesus' messianic practice expresses his freedom from the rigidity of the prevailing laws, in the name of an interpersonal humanization. He shows his awareness of his identity—that of his Father's Son—in his demand for unrestricted attachment to his message and person. His practice is expressed in terms of a liberation of the damned of this earth (the poor, the sick, social and religious outcasts) as a concretization of the presence of the Reign of God, and the realization of the Father's project. Gradually his message and demands provoke a great conflict.[3] By the end of his life Jesus is at odds with everyone in power.[4] Indeed, his life is threatened at the very start (Mark 3:6).

What is decisive for us here is the way Jesus faces any situation of conflict. He never loses his courageous, prophetic tone. Never does he lose his trust in people's capacity for conversion. He never repays in kind. And yet he is anything but unaware of the danger to his life, because he takes precautions against it, leaving Palestine for Tyre after Herod's threat (Luke 13:31–33), or hiding the night when he is in Jerusalem (John 18:2).

Jesus celebrates his Last Supper with his friends, then, in an atmosphere electric with the threat of persecution and death. And yet there is an air of joy as well. Why? First and foremost, because this meal is the anticipation and celebration of the "banquet of the Kingdom"—the eschatological moment of communion and fellowship in the good things of the Reign of God, the Reign of God that is the very core of all Jesus' preaching. "Happy is he who eats bread in the Kingdom of God," he cries (Luke 14:15; cf. Luke 22:15–18, Mark 14:25, Matt. 26:29). This is the first and basic meaning of our Eucharist, then. Wherever Jesus' supper is eaten, the Reign of God is anticipated and concretized. With us too, then, the atmosphere will be one of joy and tragedy at once. We feel the same mixture of emotions that Jesus himself felt, as he expressed it to his Apostles that night: "I have greatly desired to eat this Passover with you before I suffer" (Luke 22:15).

We have four different redactions (1 Cor. 11:23–25, Matt. 26: 26–29, Mark 14:22–25, and Luke 22:15–20). Despite the conflict, and its imminent, catastrophic resolution, there is still room for celebration. The Reign will come. It cannot be prevented. God's cause brooks no defeat. If it does not come by conversion it will come by martyrdom. The symbols of Jesus' supper are those of martyrdom: the body surrendered, the blood to be shed. There is no ignoring the sacrificial aspect of this supper. Nor does the sacrifice consist in the mere performance of a rite or celebration of a symbol. A concrete act is being accomplished: Jesus actually delivers himself, and truly dies, for love of sinners. The deed is definitive, everlastingly valid and present to God. The eucharistic sacrifice of the Church is not the daily renewal of Christ's sacrifice. Christ's sacrifice is always here. But it is here invisibly. The celebration of the Eucharist renders it visible, and sacramentalizes it—confers on it the structure of a sacrament, the sign-and-vehicle of presence and grace.

Jesus can celebrate his self-surrender in this atmosphere of death because the reality of the Reign of God, concretized and embodied this night, can never be effectively threatened or definitively impeded. Persecution, curses, death itself, only permit Christians to follow Jesus in his surrender—to make themselves a sacrifice, too, as they enter into intimate communion with God and forgive the perpetrators of the evil. To live in this spirit, the spirit of Jesus, is to enroll in the messianic community of the Reign of God. To live in this spirit, Jesus' spirit, is already to experience the presence of the heavenly banquet, already to be a new creation—now, and not only in eternity. This disposition will not deliver us from fear. It did not deliver Jesus from his mortal terror in the Garden of Olives. It abides *despite* the fear, and in the very midst of the fear, for we have adopted it through our own free decision. Not for nothing did St. Irenaeus regard the Eucharist as "the offering of the free," stamped with "the brand of liberty."[5]

WITHOUT A QUEST FOR COMMUNION, THE EUCHARIST IS AN OFFENSE TO GOD

How do today's Christians actually celebrate the Eucharist?[6] Most emphasize not the aspect of sacrificial surrender, but that of the worship and adoration of the presence of the Lord. Even theology, for centuries now, has been preoccupied with the precise manner of the eucharistic presence. What exactly happens to the bread and wine at the moment of transubstantiation (or transignification, or transfinalization)?[7] But in communities inserted into the reality of an oppressed people, the concern shifts. Now the question becomes, How is it possible worthily to celebrate the Eucharist, in a manner consonant with the character of Jesus' own Eucharist, in a world of injustice and disregard for human rights?[8] Can we afford to be satisfied with the personal aspect of worship and adoration? Will there not be some connection between eucharistic worship and a more just communion of sisters and brothers? Now we are at the heart of prophetic discourse. Now we touch the kernel of St. Paul's concern when he speaks of the Eucharist. Now we are in contact with the doctrine of Jesus himself as St. Matthew's Gospel preserves for us.

The prophets' attack on worship is devastating. What they excoriate, however, is not worship as such, but worship invoked as an alibi for the worshipers' indifference to the cry of the oppressed. The prophets cannot abide the substitution of the worship of God for concern with social injustice.[9] Here we shall do well to recall certain texts verbatim, as their validity endures undiminished to our very day.

> I hate, I spurn your feasts,
> I take no pleasure in your solemnities;

> Your cereal offerings I will not accept,
>   nor consider your stall-fed peace offerings.
> Away with your noisy songs!
>   I will not listen to the melodies of your harps.
> But if you would offer me holocausts,
>   then let justice surge like water,
>   and goodness like an unfailing stream.
>
> Amos 5:21–24

Or again:

> The Most High approves not the gifts of the godless,
>   nor for their many sacrifices does he forgive their sins.
> Like the man who slays a son in his father's presence
>   is he who offers sacrifice from the possessions of the poor.
> He slays his neighbor who deprives him of his living;
>   he sheds blood who denies the laborer his wages.
>
> Sir. 34:19–20, 22

What manner of worship does please God, then? The prophet Isaiah gives the answer:

> Releasing those bound unjustly,
>   untying the thongs of the yoke;
> Setting free the oppressed,
>   breaking every yoke;
> Sharing your bread with the hungry,
>   sheltering the oppressed and the homeless;
> Clothing the naked when you see them,
>   and not turning your back on your own.
>
> Isa. 58:6–7

This, then, is God's burning desire: "Let justice surge like water, and goodness like an unfailing stream" (Amos 5:24).[10] Jesus is very conscious of standing in the same prophetic tradition, and he cries out to the religious authorities, "If you understood the meaning of the text, 'It is mercy I desire and not sacrifice' . . . (Matt. 12:7, citing Hos. 6:6; cf. Matt. 9:13). Jesus establishes priorities. It is good to be devout. It is good to fast, and to tithe. But far more important are justice, mercy, and fidelity (Matt. 23:23). Jesus breaks with the devout religious leaders of his time—not because of their devotional practices, which are good, but because while practicing their piety these same individuals "devour the savings of widows and recite long prayers for appearance' sake" (Mark 12:38–40; cf. Luke 20:46–47). In other words, under the cloak of religious devotion they are exploiters of human beings.[11]

What is the prophets' intent here? What is Jesus' intent? To invalidate all worship? By no means. Like the prophets, Jesus is only seeking to restore truth to worship and religion. One's piety ought to be the expression of a righteous and just life. When it becomes a cloak for mechanisms of exploitation, it becomes idolatry. It is an offense against the God who loves justice and hates iniquity. Never may we permit ourselves to divorce worship from morality. It is by our ethical practice, especially where the needy are concerned, that we shall be judged by the Supreme Judge (Matt. 25:36–45). St. John recounts Jesus' washing the feet of his Apostles at the Last Supper (John 13). The first Eucharist was an event of service, an experience of radical interpersonal communion.

After these reflections we cannot escape the truth of the matter: the Eucharist cannot be celebrated in the spirit of Jesus when that celebration is unaccompanied by a hunger and thirst for justice. We betray the Eucharist, the memorial of the Lord, when we utilize it for the concealment of, or even when we merely ignore, the presence of unjust relations in the community of the faithful who celebrate and assist at that Eucharist.

The incongruity of such a "celebration" was crystal clear to Paul. The Apostle comments on divisions and injustices in the Christian community of Corinth. The community has gathered. Now some push their way forward, stuff themselves on food and besot themselves on drink, while others go hungry (1 Cor. 11:17–22). When this occurs the community has no business celebrating the Lord's supper (1 Cor. 11:20).[12] If it does, then anyone guilty of the social injustice upon which Paul is commenting, eats and drinks of the bread and the chalice of the Lord unworthily, and therefore "sins against the body and blood of the Lord" and "eats and drinks a judgment on himself" (1 Cor. 11:27, 29). Paul's concern here is the importance of authenticity in Christian communion. In order to enjoy a communion with Christ, we must enter into a communion with our brothers and sisters. But this implies a communality of goods, lest anyone suffer need. In the Acts of the Apostles, the breaking of bread always goes hand in hand with a communion of goods and union of hearts (see Acts 2:42–46, 4:32). The writer of the Letter to the Hebrews rightly admonishes us, "Do not neglect good deeds and generosity: God is pleased by sacrifices of that kind" (Heb. 13:16). Eucharistic worship, then, does not, cannot, give us a dispensation from, or replace a commitment to, justice and the quest for relations of communion with our sisters and brothers.

Wherein lies the reason for this so-intimate bond between worship and the practice of justice and of mutual sharing? Paul finds it in the Eucharist itself. In the Eucharist, says the Apostle, "You proclaim the death of the Lord until he comes!" (1 Cor. 11:26). Paul understands the "death of the Lord" in the full force of its sacrifice and surrender ("This is my body, which is for you"—1 Cor. 11:24). Jesus did not cling to his life. He made himself a gift to others. In order to communicate in Christ, then, we must do as he: become a gift to others. The expression, "Do this . . . in remembrance of me" (1 Cor. 11:24; cf. Luke 22:19 and parallels), does not mean merely, "Hold this celebration again and again." It means, "Perform the same deed of surrender as I. Give yourselves really (and not just symbolically) to others, and to the limit" (cf. John 13:1).[13] Were this attitude to prevail among us, how could the poor ever suffer hunger? How could a division between haves and have-nots ever reign in the community?

But in order to render the Eucharist authentic, it is not enough merely to seek justice. Jesus goes a step further. The celebration of the Eucharist presupposes the mending of all rents in the tissue of society. It presupposes *structural* reconciliation.

If you bring your gift to the altar and there recall that your brother has anything against you, leave your gift at the altar, go first to be reconciled with your brother, and then come and offer your gift.

Matt. 5:23–24

The theological background for this reconciliation is found in the Christian message itself, so well formulated by St. John:

> If anyone says, "My love is fixed on God,"
> yet hates his brother,
> he is a liar.
> One who has no love for the brother he has seen
> cannot love the God he has not seen.
> The commandment we have from him is this:
> whoever loves God must also love his brother.
>
> 1 John 4:20–21

We must love our neighbor with the same sweeping movement with which we love God. After all, there is really only one commandment: the commandment of love. Love of God is "veri-fied"—"made true"—in love of neighbor. Any celebration pretending to center on God, to the exclusion of mending broken relationships, will fail in its quest for God. After all, it has effectively blocked the road that infallibly leads to God: the path of love of neighbor.[14] Camilo Torres, the priest who lived the searing truth of the Gospel to the hilt and then died that that truth might live in history, exhorted his friends as follows, on June 24, 1965, in an effort to create the necessary concrete conditions for an authentic eucharistic worship: "The Christian community cannot offer the sacrifice in an authentic form if it has not first fulfilled in an effective manner the precept of 'love thy neighbor.' "[15] In terms of the exigencies of the Gospel, in order to guarantee the Christian authenticity of the Eucharist, it will not be enough that the Eucharist be put together according to dogmatic principles and ritualized according to all of the disciplinary and liturgical canons. In all respect for the ecclesial value of dogmatic determinations and canonical discipline, the Church must still honor and observe the spirit of Jesus. In the spirit of Jesus, true worship of God is realized more in the concretization of justice and the building of a community of sisters and brothers than in the formalities of a symbolic celebration.

"DO NOT GIVE WHAT IS HOLY TO DOGS"

The primitive Church was in earnest about the bond between a communion of brothers and sisters and their eucharistic worship. It frequently appropriated the admonition of the Lord, "Do not give what is holy to dogs or toss your pearls before swine" (Matt. 7:6). The second-century pagan historian Pliny testifies to the connection Christians made between their eucharistic celebration and their observance of the Gospel ethic. In a letter to the Emperor Trajan, Pliny writes that Christians in their Sunday worship "bind themselves by solemn oath not to commit theft or robbery or adultery, not to betray their word, and to return what they have borrowed."[16] The first Christian catechism, the *Didachē,* compiled between A.D. 90 and A.D. 100, in treating the Sunday Eucharist, prescribes that "anyone living in discord with another not join you before having a reconciliation, lest your sacrifice be profaned."[17] It is a matter of common knowledge that Christians who had committed sins tending to the destruction of the community, such as murder, adultery, or a public denial of their faith, were excluded from the eucharistic celebration.[18] The reason for this is to be found in the Christian conviction that the communion of the Body and Blood of the Lord has real, existential meaning only when accompanied by a communion in the social body.

This conviction was so profound that one of the prerequisites for the eucharistic communion in the first centuries was the sharing of one's possessions. St. Justin Martyr (d. 165), in one of the earliest extant testimonials to Christian eucharistic practice, recounts that on the occasion of the celebration of the Eucharist, all would bring a portion of their goods to the celebration to be offered for the succor of orphans, widows, the sick, strangers, and others who might be in need.[19] St. Cyprian of Carthage minces no words with a wealthy Christian:

If you stay as you are you cannot do good works in the Church. Do you really think you can see in the dark? With those eyes of yours crusted over with the sties of night? Never shall you behold the unhappy, the poor.

Rich and mighty one, do you think you celebrate the Lord's day, you who are too haughty to so much as cast a glance at the offering plate, you who come to church without bringing a farthing and then walk off with a part of what the poor have brought as their own offering? You had better be mindful of the widow in the Gospel.[20]

But it was not just any alms that expressed the necessary sisterly and brotherly communion. The only acceptable gift was one that actually represented the giver's participation in the communitarian life, in the Gospel spirit of a quest for unity and justice. The alms of notoriously unjust persons, those who oppressed their neighbor, were refused. A third-century document issuing from the Christian community of the South of Syria, the *Didascalia,* the "Teaching of the Twelve Apostles and the Holy Disciples of Our Redeemer," contains the following trenchant admonition: "If the poor of the Church are so poor that they can only be nourished by the alms of the unjust, then it were better they starve!"[21]

Here we see the organic link between communion with the poor and Communion in the Body of Christ. The grand, genuinely salvific sacrament is the sacrament of the poor. When we receive *that* sacrament in communion, through a loving solidarity that manifests itself in an attention to the needs of the poor, we infallibly receive Christ in communion as well—Christ concealed in the poor and identified with them (Matt. 25:40, 45: "You did it for me. . . . you neglected to do it to me"). But communion in the Eucharist does not automatically involve effective and authentic communion with Christ, although he is, of course, always present in the Eucharist. The crucial question is whether we come to the Eucharist already in possession of that broader communion with our sisters and brothers and the ecclesial community.

NEITHER POLITICAL HYPOCRISY NOR EUCHARISTIC LAXITY

But these reflections, based on the primitive fonts of our faith—Holy Scripture and the practice of the infant Church—place us on the horns of a dilemma. What are we to say of our customary celebration of the Eucharist on those civil occasions in which the celebrants are gathered in the name of diverse, if not out-and-out divergent, interests? By no means am I calling into question the theological content of the sacrament, with its effect *ex opere operato* and the Real Presence of Christ. What I am questioning is the use we make of the eucharistic celebration on these occasions. Our current practice is the outgrowth of old polemics on the manner of Christ's Presence under the eucharistic species, the sacrificial value of the Mass, and the intimate bond linking Eucharist, ministerial priesthood, and church unity. A by-product of these three dogmatic questions is the piety of the adoration of the Eucharist, the public proclamation of the Real Presence in eucharistic processions, and so on, and the exaltation of the ministerial priesthood in terms of putting together the Sacrament of the Altar. Without denying the value of these manifestations of eucharistic piety, I nevertheless think it important, precisely out of respect for the dignity of the Eucharist, to underscore certain points.

First of all we must undertake an *evangelizing process* where our eucharistic practices are concerned. By evangelization I mean a return to Jesus' original proclamation and practice, a reassimilation of the meaning he personally ascribed to those words and deeds of his that the Church preserves in his memory. As Paul recalls to the Corinthians, in the eucharistic celebration we proclaim to this world of ours the death of Jesus (1 Cor. 11:26). We announce the Christian ethos: an existence that will be a "proexistence," a life on behalf of others, a life of surrender to God's cause—his Reign— a life of service to the very poorest, as we join with them in their struggle for justice and communion, knowing full well that our solidarity with them in their struggle will mean our solidarity with them in their persecution and death. Jesus has gone before us down this path. The eucharistic supper is both the memorial and the continuous actualization of this gift of his, for he has never ceased giving the gift of himself as he surrenders to God for the sake of a total liberation of men and women. The Eucharist, then, is the sacrificial expression of our reconciliation with God and with one another. It is the *Sacramentum unitatis* par excellence. It not only expresses the union that God has already realized in us and for us, in Christ and the Spirit—it is also a force for union, generating dynamisms of oneness and unification in this torn world. We must never forget that Jesus celebrated his last meal in an atmosphere of conflict and death. But the conflict is no obstacle to the celebration. What is being celebrated is precisely the obliteration of the conflict. The conflict may not be erected into a pretext for manipulating the celebration into an expression of a nonexistent unity and reconciliation. Of course, the celebration is always in place when persons and communities are actively engaged in healing the rifts that divide them and securing a convergence that will respect the dignity of all parties.

Current practice reflects precious little concern with this aspect of the sacredness of Christian celebration. It is customary to celebrate Mass as part of massive public ceremonies. And the oppressors of the people often take the first places, just as they did in Jesus' land and time. We see persons receiving Holy Communion who lack all communion with the citizens they govern, or, rather, the subjects they dominate. They have not been elected by these citizens, and the policies they conduct are openly prejudicial to the interests of the vast impoverished masses. This is a profanation of the meaning of the Eucharist, and a scandal to all those who seek their inspiration in the Gospel of Jesus Christ. The scandal is magnified when it is committed in the presence of priests and bishops, who, by virtue of their pastoral office, ought to be proclaiming the liberative and prophetic significance of the death of Christ to the mighty of this world.

Once a collective evangelization of the entire Church, beginning with the clergy, has opened our eyes to the importance of the attitudes just described, it will be important to take certain community options consistent with the content of this evangelization. How well José M. Castillo observes:

The solution will be found not in "ecclesiastical decisions," but in "community options." We face a problem affecting the whole Church. The Church is not just clergy. It will have to be the community, therefore—

each concrete community that celebrates the Eucharist—who take responsibility for their Eucharistic celebrations and their concrete manner of "proclaiming the death of the Lord" before society.[22]

Here it will be important to develop an evangelically mature community spirit, after the model of Jesus. Jesus was most forthright when there was a question of the proclamation of the Reign and the will of the Father. But he was merciful and understanding when he encountered human weakness and sin. We too, then, must take care not to fall victim to the extremes: either the political hypocrisy that exorcises from the eucharistic community simply any type of unjust person, or the eucharistic laxity that admits simply everyone inclined to participate, regardless of the type and degree of an individual's unrighteousness. In the course of the centuries, the Church has developed a number of disciplinary norms to safeguard the sanctity of the Sacrament of the Eucharist. Even today it excludes divorced persons from the public reception of Holy Communion. Has the time not come when our Church, consistent with the level of consciousness it has reached with respect to social sin and institutional injustices that cry to heaven, ought to regulate access to the eucharistic celebration in function of this consciousness as well? Ought it not to deny such access to notorious oppressors of the people and agents of enterprises that exploit the life of these poor? The Church would not be judging the subjective culpability of the oppressor or agent, any more than it judges the subjective culpability of the divorced person whom it forbids to receive the Eucharist in public. Rather, simply in view of the degree of scandal that is objectively profaning the Eucharist in a given case, owing to its direct contrariety to the character of the Eucharist as the memorial of Jesus, the Church would enjoin certain persons from public participation in the Holy Eucharist until such time as he or she would have become the willing instrument of the reconciliation that this Jesus has achieved for us with the sacrifice of his very life.

Finally, the Church is not only the community of worship that celebrates the total liberation bestowed on us by God the Father through the death and Resurrection of his Christ and in the Power of his Spirit. The Church is also the community of historical commitment that, enlightened by the practice of Jesus and animated by the power of the eucharistic celebration, effects in the world, from a point of departure among the poor, this same integral liberation of human beings. These two aspects of Church constitute a dialectical unity. Each implies and involves the other. It should be the constant concern of the Church to maintain this unity, in the fullness of both aspects of being Church.

Like any sign, the eucharistic celebration ever retains a dimension of unfathomable obscurity. The union it symbolizes and effects is never complete. Our history continues to be scarred by all manner of breach and rupture, and this prevents the mystery of the Eucharist from ever being transparent. But the Eucharist sacramentally points to, and renders visible, Someone in whom the world is already reconciled, Someone in whom the world is already present to the plenitude of the Reign of God. This Someone is Jesus, who has died and been raised again. These are the reason why every Eucharist we celebrate has its measure of sadness and joy—a sadness and joy according to God, however, and not according to this world. As long as we live, let us safeguard the sanctity of our celebrations. Thus they will always be able to accomplish their triple purpose. They will recall for us that event of a bygone time, Jesus' surrender and total gift of himself. They will accomplish the action ever and ever to be repeated, the unification and reconciliation of human beings with one another and with God. And they will direct our gaze to that happy outcome of history when God will be fully in us and we shall be fully in God, and the universe itself will be "Eucharist"—thanksgiving.

6. How Ought We To Preach the Cross in a Crucified Society Today?

ARS THEOLOGICA PAR EXCELLENCE: THE ART OF SPEAKING OF DEATH AND THE CROSS

Few topics lend themselves so readily to ideological manipulation, to the attempt to justify the humiliation and subjugation of persons, as does the subject of death and the cross. We are all familiar with interpretations of Christ's passion in Christian piety and homiletics that exalt the cross for its own sake, to finish in the cult of pain and suffering that so paralyzes the Christian struggle with the mechanisms that produce, precisely, the cross with all of its pain.

But this ambiguity is inherent in the theme of death and the cross.[1] On the one hand, death is part and parcel of life. As such, it constitutes a neutral, innocent datum, bound up with the finitude and mortality that God has willed for his creation. But death is also the consequence of sin (Rom. 5:12, 1 Cor. 15:21–22), and is experienced as a curse, as punishment (Gen. 2:17, Gal. 3:13). The cross has two sides as well. It is the instrument of an atrocious punishment for slaves and political dissidents. Inflicted on the innocent, as on Jesus, it constitutes a political and religious crime. And it is also one of Christianity's mightiest symbols—the graphic embodiment of Christ's redemption and the Father's salvific will.

It is an art, then, and a most difficult one, to be able to speak of death and the cross in such a way that they appear for all that they are—contraventions of the project of the living God, and at the same time the price one must pay for the implementation of this project amidst our decadent history. Let me attempt to meet the challenge of this paradox now, as I enter upon an analysis of these two different levels of meaning inherent in death and the cross. If I succeed, I shall have clarified their reciprocal articulation, and thus have made a contribution to a rehabilitation of our traditional regard for death and the cross as moments of sacrifice and solidarity.

Given the inherent ambiguity of this subject, one must be constantly on the alert. How should death and the cross be proclaimed today? How should death and the cross *not* be proclaimed today? Our very faith demands that this vigilance be exercised. Our faith will not tolerate a utilization of the name of God and the symbols of his mercy to justify attitudes and situations that contravene his will. They may not be employed to mask a will to domination on the part of the mighty.

DEATH AND THE CROSS OF THE INNOCENT: HIGHEST EXPRESSION OF THE HUMAN

Let me begin by making some basic propositions.

First of all, life is ontologically mortal. Death does not suddenly appear on the scene at the close of our life. It installs itself at life's very heart. We die continuously. We waste away, spending our vital energies, consuming the moments of our time in succession until our dying is done. We die not only if someone kills us, we must die in any case. Life hosts death in its very structure. Death is our mode of being: it manifests itself in the finitude of our opportunities for living, for feeling, for understanding, for loving. We encounter such limitations in every articulation of our existence. They translate as a sense of anguish, an anguish for which there is no cure, for it is part and parcel of our *condition humaine.* Any goal we may ever achieve immediately becomes a mere step along the way to a higher objective.

But this natural mortality—natural because it is integral to the mystery of our creation—becomes our existential cross the moment we perceive the disparity between our infinite desire and its finite realization, between the principles of an unlimited *eros* and the *thanatos,* the death, which sucks all things into its gullet. We feel our "gratuity," our *etre de trop.* We can assign no reason for our existence. The human cross is planted in a spirit dimensioned for the infinite but rooted in the finite. There is an ontological *inadaequatio* here, an imbalance in our being, a mystery in human existence.

Jesus shared this human structure. Jesus "dies not only because we human beings kill, but also because we human beings die."[2] In function of this conceptualization, the preaching of the cross means the preaching of an acceptance of our mortal existence, without bitterness, but with sovereignty, and *amor fati.* It implies renunciation of pride of place, it implies a refusal of all religious and political totalitarianism, it implies a foregoing of all dogmatism and absolutism. It is an invitation to toleration, to historical patience, to the joy of the provisional. So God has willed us. We find ourselves obliged to divest ourselves of everything that pretends to be absolute in time, everything except God. We are called on to make a permanent surrender, to adopt an attitude of leavetaking with respect to all of the things and relationships of this world. The last moment of life will place us in a last, final solitude—an aloneness with ourselves and with our God. Now our dying will be complete, as the terminus of the dying process inexorably summons us to make a last surrender to Someone greater, to effectuate a complete extrapolation from our own center to the heart of God. Death calls on us to make a supreme act of love, for the perfect deed of freedom. Therefore death offers the greatest opportunity for the highest humanization. Our leavetaking of the world opens out on the opportunity of a complete assumption of God. To live, then, is not an inexorable journey into death. Rather, to die is an auspicious pilgrimage into God.

If this is our perspective, how can we allow ourselves to preach death and the cross as a biological failure and a personal trauma? We ought to be picturing death not as the end of life, but as a dimension opening out upon a future, as a new opportunity for existence offered at the end of life.[3] Even the ancients said that we are twice born, but never actually die. We are born once when we leave our mother's womb. Then we are born again in death, when we bid farewell to this cozy world of ours, to enter a greater world, where we shall greet those who traveled on this journey before us, our parents, our sisters and brothers, our relatives and friends. In dying we only take leave of this tremendous cosmic placenta, to be born to eternity. Death is not the specter of the final tragedy, but a vision of benediction, of the opportunity of a new life that will be more real, and more really full, than the old one could ever have been. The important thing is not what we leave behind, but what we receive, what is unveiled before our eyes. To die is not to lose our life, but to gain it in more perfect, more vigorous form.

THE AGONY OF DEATH AND THE CROSS: THE STIGMA OF SIN

Death, natural though it surely is in its organic links with the mortal structure of life, is nevertheless not experienced as something natural. Normally we experience death as an assault on nature, and therefore as unnatural. We feel our existence torn and broken. Ontological anguish is transformed into terror, into fear and trembling. It is agonizing to bid farewell to the bonds that concretize our being-in-the-world together with others. Death appears under the mask of a terrifying ghost. We fail to integrate it into our life project. It comes on the scene precisely as the destroyer of all of the interrelationships we call life. St. Paul tells us that death as we actually experience it, death in the concrete, has been brought on by sin (Rom. 5:12). Sin not only severs our umbilical cord to God. It also sears us inwardly. It affects our inward identity. As St. Paul says, "I am weak flesh sold into the slavery of sin. I cannot even understand my own actions. I do not do what I want to do but what I hate. . . . Who can free me from this body under the power of death" (Rom. 7:14–15, 24).

Jesus of Nazareth, a human being (whose humanity is that of the eternal Son) shares this situation. Amidst "loud cries and tears" (Heb. 5:7), he looks death full in the face. He tells his friends straight out, "My heart is filled with sorrow to the point of death" (Mark 14:34). His "soul is troubled" (John 12:27), and in his terror he sweats a sweat "like drops of blood" (Luke 22:44).

The assumption of our battered humanity (our flesh) by the eternal Son forges a bond of solidarity with him in our anguish. New Testament theological reflection identifies Jesus as "the Lamb of God who takes away the sin of the world" (John 1:29), recalling the prophecy of Isaiah (Isa. 53:11). Paul radicalizes the sense of this solidarity in his scandalous assertion that Jesus became "sin" for us (2 Cor. 5:21), became "a curse for us" (Gal. 3:13). Because of sin, the natural isolation of death, which objectively affords us the opportunity for a surrender to, and encounter with, the fountainhead of life itself, is transformed into a dereliction, an abyss, a vacuum. Jesus willed to descend to the very hell of this abandonment. He willed to experience, in his inmost being, the consequences of sin—the expelling of the presence of God from the horizon of life. This is the meaning of his cry on the cross, in solidarity with all sinners: "My God, my God, why have you forsaken me" (Mark 15:34).[4]

But death's anguish is overpowered by the life of faith—by the discipleship and following of Jesus. The Christian life assimilates God's project for life in such a way as to exorcise the terror of death. The Christian life grasps that life is called to life, so that we Christians actually live and experience death as a "sister" who takes us by the hand and leads us into the house of eternal life. But this presupposes a life journey of faith, and radical trust. Here again, Jesus is our example. In the midst of his mortal terror, Jesus can still say, *"Abba* [O Father], . . . let it be as you would have it, not as I" (Mark 14:36). And his last utterance is one of trust and surrender: "Father, into your hands, I commend my spirit" (Luke 23:46).

For Christian faith, the preaching of death and the cross is an appeal for a grasp of the realism of our sinful condition. The sin of the world and our own personal sin have power to manifest death in its macabre aspect, in its quality of solitude and abandonment.[5] It is second nature to us (a second nature, according to Pascal, shaped by the history of sin) to be subject to this splintering anguish. It is our sinful nature. An acceptance of this reality, with a humble conscience and an openness to the divine mercy, associates us with all of the sinners of history. Thus we are incorporated into Christ's own act of solidarity, and in this way we are helped to redeem the sin in ourselves. Not even Christ escaped the sinful condition of our flesh (2 Cor. 5:21). Even Christ died alone, just as we. And because he died for us, we need no longer regard ourselves as abandoned, however agonizingly we may experience and suffer the silence of God.

But we must not preach death and the cross as if they "had the last word"—as if the power and terror of sin alone prevailed in us. The Christian experience is consistent with Christian belief. The Christian experience gives birth to the new human being within us, that woman or man who is free of the fear of death, and reintegrates death within the broader phenomenon of life. Paul's articulation of the two regimes, sin and grace, death and life, in his Letter to the Romans is a stroke of genius (chapters 5–7). In the final assessment, he explains, sin is subordinated to grace and death is ordered to life: "Despite the increase of sin, grace has far surpassed it, so that, as sin reigned through death, grace may reign by way of justice leading to eternal life, through Jesus Christ our Lord" (Rom. 5:20–21). Once again, trust reigns supreme. We do not suffer in vain.

DEATH AND THE CROSS AS CRIME: DENUNCIATION AND CONDEMNATION

The presence of sin as a destructive historical force is manifest in the thousands of crosses human beings prepare for one another. The crucified are legion. Nearly every human being on the face of the Earth hangs on some cross. This cross is wicked, and an abomination to God. A horrible, persistent cross hunches the shoulders of Latin America's subjugated black and Amerindian cultures. This cross is an injustice, and has produced a veritable demographic hecatomb. According to Cook-Simpson, in 1519 there were 11,000,000 Indians living in Mexico; by 1607 the number had fallen to 2,014,000.[6] Wars, disease, and incredibly barbarous oppressions had decimated the dominated population. Nor has this process ever been reversed. Millions upon millions of the downtrodden in Latin America continue to eke out their crucified existence, subsisting on starvation wages, struggling in working conditions that cut their lives off in their youth, languishing in hygienic situations that slaughter some forty million persons annually. Other persons and groups writhe on the cross of discrimination simply because they happen to be female, or sick, or poor, or black, or homosexual, or Marxist, or by reason of some other criterion of exclusion and social death.

In his proclamations, as in his practice, Jesus makes a preferential option for all of these outcasts. Through him is inaugurated the Reign of God, which is to be a regime of the liberation of the oppressed. Be they oppressed by blindness, by imprisonment, or by the threat of death (cf. Luke 4:17–21, Matt. 11:2–6), these are the privileged members of the Reign. There is no denying that the historical Jesus made this preferential option for the very neediest.[7] His option is the reason for his holy wrath against the injustices of this world. His option involves an act of political love. Jesus sees that the reality around him contradicts his Father's plan. If this reality is overcome, this is a sign that the Reign of God is in our midst (Luke 7:22). And so he hurls his invectives against the perpetrators of the injustices—the rich (Luke 6:24), the greedy (Luke 12:15), those who fail in solidarity (Matt. 25:33–46). His option translates into a practice of liberation, beginning with a focus on life's infrastructure: hunger is slain, diseases are healed, the dead are raised, and a new social relationship is established. Now the ties that knit society will no longer be based on the interests of power, but on gift and universal acceptance. Now we shall have a society that accepts all persons on an equal footing, even the "least ones," even our enemies (Luke 6:35–36).

What does it mean to preach death and the cross in this context? It means that we must become prophets. It means proclamation and denunciation—*anuncio e denuncia*. We must *proclaim* the judgment of God that tears the mask from the face of this antireality, this disorder masquerading as order, this "social balance" that is the sheer dominance of one class, which uses the apparatus of state to realize its interests while the underclasses foot the bill. We must *denounce* injustice as cruelty, poverty as a process of impoverishment of the people, and wealth as possessions heaped up on the backs of the masses. There are times when Christian leaders should be more prophets than shepherds. Pastors, shepherds, see to the mediations, saving where they can, balancing the forces in tension, comforting and aiding the bleeding sheep, going in search of the one that is lost, and taking care lest fat sheep gobble up the fodder intended for the thin ones. Prophets live two radical fidelities at once. One is to God, in whose name they proclaim and denounce. The other is to the people, the poor, on whose behalf they raise their voices and utter their cry. Prophets smite the wolves with their crooks, denouncing their ruses and telling the whole truth, despite its stinging like salt on a raw wound. But bishops are not only pastors, not only shepherds. Bishops are prophets, as well—teachers of the full truth. Theirs is the duty to proclaim not only the truth about God, Christ, the Church, and human beings, but the truth about poverty as well, the truth about the spoliation of the people and the imposition of authoritarian, antipopular regimes. The crosses that martyrize the lowly and defenseless must be denounced and condemned. God abominates them, Christ struggled against them, and those with a sense of humanity reject them. Bishops will be found on the same side.

There is an attitude, a way of proclaiming death and the cross, that must be avoided at all costs. There is a preaching of the cross which, without any such intent on the part of the preachers, ends by legitimating abominations, or representing them as a providence of the will of God. This is *fatalism*. Fatalism maintains that there is simply no escaping the suffering and death that pervade our history. The lethal flaw of fatalism lies in its abstraction and insensitivity. If fails to distinguish between that suffering and death that are part and parcel of life—the suffering and death that we considered earlier, issuing from the finite structure of existence—and a suffering and death needlessly, wickedly inflicted by the strong on the weak. Furthermore, fatalism removes all hope. It freezes history. For fatalism, history can only be the endless repetition of the same. And so the human being is reduced to helplessness and impotency. The mighty are great lovers of fatalism. The permanence of the status quo is to their benefit, of course, because it is they who control history. It is they who prevent the poor from shaking off their chains and becoming the agents of a more worthy destiny.

Another attitude tending to legitimate death and the cross consists in *pessimism* and *cynicism.* Cynics and pessimists are the hardhearted enemies of their own humanity, refusing to believe in the possibility of overpowering dehumanizing relationships. They ridicule Christian believers, and even manage to cite passages from the Bible in their efforts to disarm the libertarian spirit. They love to quote the saying of Jesus "The poor you always have with you (John 12:8). As we know, Jesus' meaning here is not that there will always be poor, let alone that God wills their poverty, but that we must never neglect the interests of the poor, that we must never turn our backs on the challenge to join the battle against poverty.

Finally, no less mistaken and pernicious is the attitude that exalts death and the cross as fonts of new life and light in themselves. The champions of this view are likely to repeat, without due reference to mediation and context, the declaration in Hebrews that "without the shedding of blood there is no forgiveness" (Heb. 9:22). There are those who would blasphemously conclude that people must therefore be killed in order that they or others may have life, or that suffering is pleasing to God. Jesus had to die, we hear (cf. John 18:14, Luke 24:26), in virtue of the Father's eternal dispensation. But statements such as these in Scripture have a very precise meaning, which we shall presently discuss, and it is not legitimate to make use of them to manufacture a cult of pain and death, or to perpetuate the crucifixions by which we offend God and render the already painful journey of the humiliated and the wronged of our history more excruciating still. Death and the cross are not directly willed or loved by God. They are not directly pleasing to him. On the contrary, of themselves they represent a cancellation of his project of life, the negation of his will to exalt the meaning of creation.[8]

DEATH AND THE CROSS EMBRACED AS THE PRICE OF THEIR DEFEAT

A prophet arises, proclaims the demands of the Reign of God, and denounces the injustice, the crosses, the violent death, meted out by the agents of sin. That prophet can count on persecution, curses, imprisonment, torture, and death. No prophet, yesterday or today, is likely to die in bed. *Prophet* here need not mean an individual. It may mean an entire institution, such as the Church that has emerged from Medellín and Puebla. An institution, too, can prophetically denounce the antievangelical character of the poverty and misery in which so many millions of our sisters and brothers in Latin America are forced to live out their lives.[9] In all serenity, such an institution will recognize that the stance it has taken is bound to entail incomprehension on the part of the ruling classes, and the whole national security state, and thus occasion a vicious persecution.[10]

Death and the cross go ever hand in hand with any new project launched as an alternative to a prevailing social structure. In our case the prevailing social structure is based on a peripheral capitalism, managed by and profiting the rich and marginalizing the vast masses of our people. No sooner is a thoroughgoing analysis of the causes of our underdevelopment undertaken, no sooner are the mechanisms of exploitation, of accumulation, on one side and misery on the other, pointed out, than the individuals and groups undertaking the analysis or doing the pointing-out are accused of "Marxism." Now they can be framed. Now they are subversives. All one need do is to join forces with the oppressed in an attempt to develop an alternative project, and to organize social practices calculated to implement that project, in order to be slandered as an "enemy of law and order," and "unpatriotic." Then, as the perpetrator of a dastardly deed, one may be persecuted with impunity, even arrested and tortured, unless one is simply made to "disappear"—that is, be murdered—because one is a "threat to the common good."[11]

There is a death and cross, then, that emerge as the consequence of a committed effort to remove death and the cross from the shoulders of the crucified. There is a death and cross that emerge from the effort to confine the reign of death and curtail the harvest of so many lives, especially innocent lives.

The *inflicted* death and cross are criminal. Jesus warns, "This generation will have to account for the blood of all the prophets shed since the foundation of the world" (Luke 11:50). The death shrieks of entire groups, whose only transgression has been their commitment to the gestation of a more humane world for all human beings, resound down through the ages, and rise to the ears and heart of God. To suffer thus, to be murdered thus, is to fall heir to the "Beatitude of Persecution," the blessed legacy of those persecuted for the sake of righteousness (Matt. 5:10). Here is a truly honorable, worthy death (Heb. 11:38).

Franz Kafka wrote the following significant words when the British in India imprisoned Gandhi in 1922:

Now it's plain that Gandhi's movement will win. . . . Without martyrs every movement degenerates into a pressure group of ordinary fortune-hunters. The river becomes a pool in which all thoughts of the future decay. For ideas—like everything else in the world which has a super-personal value—only live by sacrifices.[12]

Historically, Jesus' cross was judicial murder, and this is how it must be regarded. It was the result of his having preached his message of supreme hope and practiced it. His liberative preaching and practice constituted a painful thorn in the side of the religious, sociopolitical, and ideological establishment. Jesus actually had to stand trial twice, once for alleged crimes against religion—for blasphemy and false prophecy—and once for political crimes as a subversive and guerrilla. Such was the view of Jesus entertained by the agents of prevailing authority. In conditions of such stubborn rejection by the ruling classes, Jesus had no alternative but to accept his persecution, torture, and the death sentence. Well do the gospel texts say that Jesus "must die" (John 19:7; cf. 19:14–16)—that "the Messiah ha[s] to undergo all this" (Luke 24:26). But the "necessity" was not a transcendent one, and we may not permit ourselves to regard it as such. Nor was it a "necessity" of some sadistic plan concocted by the Father. Jesus' death was a *historical* necessity. Given the conditions of nonconversion and rejection by which he was surrounded, if Jesus were to be faithful to his Father, to himself, and to the human beings in whom he had aroused such radical hopes of the Reign of God, he would have to reckon with the inevitability of persecution and a violent end.

God did not directly will the death of Jesus. God is a God of the living. His plan is life and love. But God willed Jesus' fidelity, and Jesus' fidelity was such that it could bring him to death on a cross, for it meant love to the limit (John 13:1). God willed Jesus' death, then, but only indirectly, only as implicit in the radical fidelity that dignifies a person, that loyalty that demonstrates consistency, faith, and the steadfast conviction that one has espoused God's own cause of truth and justice. The death inflicted on Jesus was a crime, then (Acts 2:23: "You even made use of pagans to crucify and kill him"; Acts 3:15: "You put to death the Author of life").

The Old Testament Songs of the Suffering Servant, which may well have helped Jesus of Nazareth to understand the course of events in his life, unveil this mortal dialectic.[13] The Servant is elected by God to establish righteousness and justice on Earth (Isa. 42:1–4)—to restore the land and refashion the people (Isa. 49:8). But his mission will make him a sufferer. Now he will be the victim of a frenzied persecution at the hands of a group who consider him the dregs of humanity, and who will do their utmost to see that his remains lie with those of the rest of the villains (Isa. 53:3–12).

How, then, ought we to preach death and the cross? If we proclaim the historical project conceived in the design of the Father and first preached by Jesus himself, and if we are willing to put our lives on the line, as Jesus did, and so construct society according to the inspirations of evangelical practice—then we must count on the lot of the Suffering Servant. We shall have to pay the price that Jesus paid. There are those who will stand against all change, there are those who will be insensitive to any appeals for justice for the poor, there are those who will use violence against the builders of new sociohistorical relations. Christian baptism comports a sharing in the death of the Lord (Rom. 6:3–4). This sharing need not be merely spiritual. It can be brutally physical. There is a price to pay for joy, and one must be willing to pay that price in all awareness and realism. The Reign forges ahead, engulfed in a struggle with the Anti-Reign, that producer of death and crosses.

How ought we *not* to proclaim the death and cross of Christ? We must not project them as fated realities. We must not proclaim them as implementations of a suprahistorical drama, a deadly game between God and the devil. This would exempt from their human responsibilities the religious authorities, the Pharisees, who had closed themselves off from Jesus; Judas, who betrayed him; and the civil authorities, who moved against him in a second trial. Biblical expressions such as "The Son of Man is going to be delivered into the hands of men who will put him to death" (Mark 9:31) must be understood in a framework of earthly, historical causalities, in a framework of the conflict provoked by Jesus' demands, message, and practice. There comes a time when martyrdom alone—the sacrifice of one's life—does justice to life, and keeps faith with God's cause. That time came for Jesus.

DEATH AND THE CROSS SUFFERED AS SACRIFICE ON BEHALF OF THOSE WHO PRODUCE THEM

What must we do when we are the innocent victims of injustice, torture, and the cross? A number of attitudes offer themselves to the free decision of human freedom.

A first possible attitude is one of *revolt.* The spirit of rebellion may reveal a final human dignity that refuses to accept humiliation. The rebel prefers a glorious death to a shameful survival, and there are many who come to this point of desperation. The guilty ones here are not so much those who so stubbornly refuse to yield, but rather those who have forced them to this extremity. Rebellion, however, does not overcome the cross. It succumbs to it.

Another possible attitude is one of *resignation*. Those who simply resign themselves to their unjust, inflicted death and cross reason that, because they cannot avoid the suffering confronting them, they should accept it. These may well preserve their interior sovereignty. But they surrender to the cross. The cross emerges the victor, and continues to rend human beings' existence. The resigned have neither the courage of a rebel nor the powerful patience of a Job. Once again on the face of the Earth, truth and justice go down in defeat. Once again the cross has conquered.

A third attitude—and the only really worthy, dignifying, and exalting one in the face of death and the cross—is that of *acceptance*. Death and the cross are still real, still inflicted, still inevitable—but suddenly they are welcome. We see that death and the cross need not have the last word. Thus we find ourselves able to accept them as an expression of love. We embrace them as a way of proclaiming our love for, and communion with, the very ones who have perpetrated this horrible evil. In this cross we find the strength to experience a healing, a reconciliation with the very persons who have caused the catastrophic wound and breach. This is not a refined escapism, or a supersophisticated transfiguration of the spirit of vengeance burning within us. If it were, we would be bitter. Instead, we love.

This attitude of acceptance springs from the profound, trusting conviction that only love and forgiveness will ever reestablish the harmony of a broken creation. Love represents the meaning of all life, even the lives of those who hate others so much that they fashion crosses for them. In these, too, love is the unifying force, and that love cries out with all its might, so that no historical sin on Earth can quench it for good. In forgiving, in welcoming an inflicted cross and death by our own free decision, and yet eliminating a distorted motivation such as the satisfaction of the pleasure principle through a kind of masochism, we lead history toward its ultimate atonement, a reconciliation that actually includes mutual enemies.

In this approach to death and the cross, the ultimate torment emerges as *sacrifice*—something onerous and repugnant (as Jesus experienced it in Gethsemane: Mark 14:32–42, Heb. 5:7)—but something we accept nonetheless, on the strength of the love we bear our enemies, and in the hope of a communion beyond all compensation. Love like that is a most precious expression of faith. It embraces good for its own sake, it transcends a utilitarian faith that harbors some hidden selfish motive. Thus it rises above any psychological, or pietistic, or even edifying dimension. Reaction itself goes by the board, displaced by an active comprehension of the structure of life, which nurtures itself only on what is life-producing, as are love, forgiveness, and this marvelous acceptance that vaults the wall thrown up by sin.

The Suffering Servant of Isaiah lived this dimension of perfect liberty:

> It was our infirmities that he bore,
>   our sufferings that he endured.
> . . . He was pierced for our offenses,
>   crushed for our sins. . . .
> Because he surrendered himself to death
>   and was counted among the wicked;
> And he shall take away the sins of many,
>   and win pardon for their offenses.
>
> Isa. 53:4–5, 12

All of this he bore "though he had done no wrong nor spoken any falsehood" (Isa. 53:9; cf. 1 Pet. 2:22).

Arrested, tortured, and sentenced to die on the cross, Jesus had this liberative attitude in the highest degree. It was not death he sought, but the Reign of God, the conversion of human beings. When the cross was inflicted on him, when his extermination faced him through no fault of his own, he did not revolt ("In his own body he brought your sins to the cross"—1 Pet. 2:24), but could say, in all serenity, "No one takes [my life] from me; I lay it down freely" (John 10:18). Death presents Jesus with the opportunity to surrender his life to those who condemned him and then forgive them. Properly speaking, our redemption in Jesus Christ is found neither in his cross, nor in his blood, nor in his death. Instead, we are redeemed by Jesus' attitude of love, surrender, and forgiveness. But it was not only his death that was loving, surrendering, and forgiving. It was his whole life. Jesus' entire existence was a "proexistence"—an existence of service to others. It is Jesus' whole life, then—and, in supreme form, his death, as the organic outgrowth of his life—that is redemptive for us. His death is the crystallization and maximal expression of his life as service (Luke 22:27) and love to the end (John 13:1).

The Christian way to preach death and the cross is to invite men and women to exercise the capacity residing within them never to leave off loving, cost what it may. The greatest sacrifices will be required. But the shadows of Earth will never eclipse the sun for good. It is important, too, to avoid the moralism of those who would, with all good intent, inflict the cross on their fellow human beings without an accompanying effort to show them that the intrinsic goodness of this cross resides in its expression of human freedom and universal communion. This does not render death and the cross legitimate. They continue to be crimes. But now the crime fails to murder meaning—fails to isolate itself from all rational sense whatsoever. Through our exercise of our freedom we effect a conversion of meaning: by taking up our cross of our own free will, we turn to the criminal in forgiveness and reconciliation. Now the road is open to a meaning over and above the raw meaning of injustice that resides in the cross in any case. Only in this perspective does the cross appear in its authentic character as redemptive and totally liberative.

DEATH AND THE CROSS ACCEPTED AS AN EXPRESSION OF SOLIDARITY WITH THE CRUCIFIED OF HISTORY

There is yet another way for us to invest death and the cross with meaning. We may accept them out of love and solidarity—

solidarity with the crucified of our history. We who are not persecuted, we who are not threatened with death, may nonetheless
throw in our lot with those who do live under persecution and the
threat of death. Now we bring that same persecution and threat
of death upon ourselves, as we offer our crucified sisters and
brothers support and aid, comfort and consolation. Thousands of
Christians, along with countless other men and women who take
up their cross in this fashion, embrace all manner of sacrifice and
limitation in their lives for the purpose of identifying with their
wronged sisters and brothers. Some confront the menaces of the
Amazon rain forest. Others burn themselves out in leprosariums.
Still others immerse themselves in the inhuman conditions of our
urban ghettos. There are those who go to live in the squalor of a
seaport red light district. All of these, by reason of their option,
suffer hunger, disease, and an early death, to say nothing of the
deaths they must die in this life. Suffering does no one any good.
The cross always crucifies. But there is a grandeur in this deed of
solidarity, and that grandeur is at once human and divine. A
preferential option for the poor comes down to this: someone who
is not poor becomes poor, in order to identify with the poor and
together with them overcome their poverty—and thus to move, all
together, in the direction of justice and a communion of sisters and
brothers.

The songs of the Suffering Servant resound with these same
redemptive chords. After all, "It was our infirmities that he bore,
our sufferings that he endured" (Isa. 53:4), our guilt that he carried
on his shoulders (Isa. 53:11). In striking a Covenant with his
people, God himself became *pathetic,* in the etymological sense of
assuming the *pathos,* the passion and suffering, of the people.[14]
God's incarnation manifests all of his empathy with, and sympathy for, this twisted humanity. God takes on our sinful fleshliness,
along with its consequences in history in terms of our frailty, the
straitened conditions of our lives, our violence, our refusal to
understand one another, and our death. Through the incarnation
of the Son, and out of pure gratuity, God makes this antireality
to be his own reality (Rom. 5:10, 15). Now God himself is cursed

with the cursed, condemned with the condemned, and crucified with the crucified. Let us make no attempt to dehistoricize the causes that led Jesus to his death. Rather let us see how, despite these causes, indeed immersed in these causes, God the Son accepted his condemnation as a way of entering into solidarity with the condemned of history. This same disposition on the part of his disciples will always demonstrate the superabundance of a love that simply cannot be overcome by the mechanisms of hatred that pervade our history.

God's sympathy for the wronged of this world has never waned. The supreme Judge becomes hungry with the starving, naked with the despoiled, and a prisoner with the imprisoned (Matt. 25:31–46). But this is a solidarity that implies reciprocity, and this is the basis of discipleship—the following of Jesus as the fullest way to live the Christian life. Now all sufferers may feel their oneness with the one who suffered the most, Jesus Christ. The scourged, tortured Christs of our popular piety depict this solidarity and reciprocity most graphically. Christ is represented as a slave lashed to the block and tortured. Christ is identified with the crucified of history. But conversely, the people see themselves portrayed in this suffering, dying Christ as well. In their marginalization and suffering, we behold a people who constitute a latter-day Suffering Servant, the Body of Christ torn by an unjust passion that cries out for redemption. In the measure that this impoverished, Christian people accepts its passion, not for any love of suffering but for love of Christ, who suffered too, it transforms itself into the Suffering Servant of very history, in whom Christ continues to suffer, continues to be tortured and crucified, until the history of the Anti-Reign is ended.

To preach death and the cross in a genuinely Christian manner is to invite our fellow Christians to embrace this powerful, revolutionary love, which is an identification with sufferers such that we actually join them in their struggle with the mechanisms that produce crosses. What we must *not* do is preach death and the cross for their own sake. The cruel and inhuman condition of these Suffering Servants does not call us first and foremost to contemplation. This situation calls us first and foremost to liberative action. We hear the cry of the starving, "I want to live!" and our response is the deed of solidarity. We bend all our heart and soul to the creation of human conditions for all humankind.

DEATH AND THE CROSS AS LOCUS AND MOMENT OF THEIR OWN DEFEAT: RESURRECTION AS VICTORY OVER DEATH AND THE CROSS

Theologically considered, Resurrection is not the sudden appearance of a new life in place of the old one after we die on the cross. No, the option whereby we accept life's mortality with equanimity as we share the lot of the sufferers, as we embrace the consequences of their struggle against their crosses, as we sacrifice ourselves on behalf of those who torture and kill so that we may be able to maintain with them at least that minimal communion called forgiveness, already possesses within itself a degree of vital intensity that death is helpless to overwhelm. Here is a life that perseveres. Here is a life that storms straight to the heart of death and returns triumphant. The proof is in Jesus' Resurrection. Here at last we begin to comprehend. It is not for nothing that St. John presents Jesus' Crucifixion and Resurrection in continuity as his hour. The moment Jesus emptied himself altogether and surrendered in trust to his Father, life, human and divine, attained in him its plenitude. This is Jesus' Resurrection. This is the locus and moment of the establishment of the Reign of God. Here we behold that Reign at long last, authentic and entire in the person of Jesus. It is in this wise that the Resurrection unveils for us the meaning that lies hidden in a life surrendered and sacrificed for others. A life lived in this manner can only lead to life. Or better, a life lived in this manner must generate life in its highest expression.

This is what St. John is insinuating in his intentionally ambiguous formula, "Then he bowed his head, and delivered over his spirit" (and his Spirit) (John 19:30). Jesus "delivered over his spirit" in the sense of genuinely dying, and not merely seeming to, as would soon be the claim of certain persons wishing to deny the

Resurrection but confronted by overwhelming evidence that Jesus was alive. But Jesus also "delivered over his Spirit" (*Paredōken to pneuma,* and not *ethēken tēn psychēn*), in the sense of delivering to us the Font of true life that is the Holy Spirit himself. Thus death and the cross are completely detraumatized, transformed into the wellspring of redemption and the generator of the new human being.

Thus as we reach the end of the crucifying course of our lives, we may make Revelation's laughing words our own: "There shall be no more death or mourning, crying out or pain"—we should say, no more cross—"for the former world has passed away" (Rev. 21:4).

7. How Ought We To Preach the Resurrection in a World Under Threat of Collective Death?

"What about Christ?" One of Kafka's friends interrupted the conversation. The great Czech writer's reply was barely audible. "This is the chasm of light," he all but whispered. "We have to close our eyes or we'll fall."

Kafka was giving expression to the basic reaction of all who have ever felt the impact of the event of Jesus' Resurrection. Here indeed is a "chasm of light"—a mystery that, like all mysteries, forces us to think, importunes us to decipher the human drama in another key.

In times gone by, the Apostles testified to an explosion of light and meaning. And the flashes have shot down through history until they have reached our own day with the same dazzle. How easy it is to feel the same sensation that Paul felt on the road to Damascus when he met the Risen One in person (Gal. 1:11–2:10; Acts 9:1–9)! This is the sensation registered so directly by Kafka and reported to us.

The question of the Resurrection has a new relevance today. There is no denying we live under the impact of the threat of a nuclear holocaust of all humanity. The notion of the end of the world is entirely secularized now. Not only God can put an end to human history, as has always been believed. Now suddenly the

These questions raised in this chapter are addressed in greater depth on the exegetical, anthropological, and theological levels in Leonardo Boff, *Vida para alem da morte*, 8th ed. (Petrópolis, Brazil: Vozes, 1983) and Leonardo Boff, *A ressurreição de Cristo—A nossa ressurreição na morte*, 6th ed. (Petrópolis, Brazil: Vozes, 1984).

decision as to our survival and that of our planet lies in our own hands. A dramatic, absurd denouement for us all can become reality. In this context, Christians draw from the treasury of their faith a hope in something beyond the catastrophe. After all, out of the ashes of the personal trajectory of one man—Jesus of Nazareth—the supreme form of human life has shot up like a star. Resurrection functions as the translation of this altogether surprising event.

DEATH: THE LAST WORD NO LONGER

Christianity lives and survives by virtue of its faith in Christ's Resurrection. With this everything stands or falls. Paul says this, in so many words: "And if Christ has not been raised . . . your faith is empty too. Indeed we should then be exposed as false witnesses of God. . . . If our hopes in Christ are limited to this life only, we are the most pitiable of men" (1 Cor. 15:14–15, 19). But if Christ has been raised, then death no longer has the last word. Christ is only first in line, and the rest of us shall be raised from the dead with him. We shall rise with him! The explosion of light is transformed into an explosion of joy. In response to the daily experience of our mortality, and in response to the philosophers of mortality, we can retort, laughing, We do not live to die, for we die to be raised!

But how may we verify, with the greatest possible rigor, the truth of this unique event in the history of human beings? It will be crucial to provide warranty for our glad demeanor. We must ensure the foundations of this incredible hope of ours. No wonder, then, that the texts reporting the Resurrection of Christ in the New Testament have been subjected to the most minute philological, historicocritical, structuralistic, and so on, scrutiny. The testimonials themselves are most complex, and the results of the examination not very inspiring. But they are sufficiently firm to sustain, in the face of the demands of reason and the skepticism of history, the assertions of the Christian community.

In most compendious terms, we can say, Faith in the Resurrection is based on the testimony of the Apostles, who bear witness to two phenomena: the empty tomb and the apparitions of a living Jesus. No one saw the Resurrection itself. They saw only Jesus, raised. Indeed, the empty tomb of itself constitutes no overwhelming proof of the Resurrection. Of itself it admits of various interpretations, one of which is actually alluded to in the texts of the New Testament itself—that of the theft of Jesus' body (Matt. 28:13).

No, the basis of the faith in the Resurrection is the apparitions of the Risen One to the disciples. Here we are dealing not with some "visions" that we could interpret as subjective extrojections on the part of persons with an interest in the person of Jesus. These are real apparitions. That is, they are the result of an action originating in Jesus and terminating in the disciples, not vice versa. This action strikes them with surprise. It registers as a reality that overflows their subjectivity on every side. Its effect is to remove the ambiguities of the empty tomb and transform the tomb into a sign and testimonial of the Resurrection as event.

Initially the New Testament writers sought to domesticate, conceptually and linguistically, this event of infinite meaning via recourse to two stock categories of the theologies of Jesus' time: that of *exaltation* and that of *Resurrection.*

Post-Exilic Judaism entertained the notion of a Suffering Just One, persecuted and humiliated by human beings but exalted—raised by God to glory. This notion furnished the theoretical framework for an understanding of Jesus' new life. Surely God had exalted the One who had so lowered himself, who had been so courageous in the encounter with the cross and death. In St. Peter's discourses in Acts we find expressions such as, "You even made use of pagans to crucify and kill him. God . . . raised him up again" (Acts 2:23–24); "exalted at God's right hand" (Acts 2:33); "he whom God has exalted at his right hand" (Acts 5:31; cf. 3:13–15).

The other category utilized by the disciples in expressing their faith in Jesus' new life was that of Resurrection. Broad strata of late Judaism awaited a Resurrection of the dead at the end of the ages. In Jesus the disciples saw the beginning of the end, the realization of an eschatological expectation, an event to be realized in the fullness of the ages: the complete transfiguration of the spiritual and corporeal earthly life of the Crucified One. They expressed this event in terms of a Resurrection. This interpretation of the glorious outcome of Jesus' life, an interpretation in terms of Resurrection, gradually came to replace the first category, the notion of exaltation. Exaltation, in the face of a denial of this manner of transfiguration on the part of Jew and Greek alike, now emerged as insufficient. It was no longer quite adequate to express the reality. The category of Resurrection had the advantage of accentuating the real transfiguration of the earthly reality of Jesus, including the corporeal aspect of that reality. Hence the Christian creed, surely the most primitive: "The Lord has been raised! It is true! He has appeared to Simon" (Luke 24:34).

A rigorous analysis of the foundational texts permits us to conclude that Jesus' Resurrection is not the product of the faith of the primitive community. The case is the other way around. We are dealing with an impact proceeding from the transfigured Jesus, and forcing itself on the disciples. It is scarcely a matter of theological creativity on the part of a few enthusiasts of the Nazarene. Extraordinary phenomena occurring after the Crucifixion obliged the Apostles to attest and confess, Jesus, to our perplexity and terror, has risen from the dead! It is true!

RESURRECTION: A UTOPIA COME TO LIFE

Once the faith event has received adequate warranty, what does the Resurrection signify in the context of Jesus' earthly life and Crucifixion? Altogether compendiously, once more, I must say, As Jesus' death and cross are the organic outcome of his life, so too the Resurrection signifies the fulfillment of his earthly meaning and life. The Resurrection renders his life full truth. The Resurrection leaves nothing to be desired where a confirmation of his message regarding the Reign of God is concerned.

A prophet arises in Galilee. Jesus of Nazareth, little by little revealed to be God in human condition, lifts his voice and proclaims, "The time of hope is accomplished. The new order willed by God is about to burst upon our heads. Change your way of thinking and acting. Believe this wonderful news" (cf Mark 1:15; Matthew 4:17, in free translation).

Jesus' message sums up the utopian dream of every heart: the overcoming, for good, of this alienated, subjected world. "The Reign of God!" is the battle cry of the prophet of Nazareth. We find it 122 times in the Gospels, 90 times on Jesus' lips. Translated into the code of our secular comprehension, it signifies a total structural revolution of the foundations of the world, introduced by God.

Reign of God denotes not so much something interior or spiritual, nor indeed something coming from without or from above, nor again something to be hoped for beyond this world or after death. The Reign of God cannot be privatized in any particular region of the human being, such as in the soul, or in some manner of spiritual goods, or in the Church. The Reign of God is all-embracing, proclaiming the deliverance of every human and cosmic reality from all sin—from the sin of poverty, from the sin of starvation, from the sin of dehumanization, from the sin of the spirit of vengeance, and from the sin of the rejection of God.

But there is more. All of this human and cosmic reality must also be delivered to its fulfillment—a plenitude that eye has never seen, ear never heard, nor heart ever dreamed. This is how we are to understand Jesus' assertion "My kingdom does not belong to this world" (John 18:36). The meaning here is that the Reign of God is not of the structure of this world of sin, but of the structure of God in the objective sense: it is God who will intervene (via the mediations he himself will select), and who will heal in its root the whole of reality, raising this world from old to new.

Jesus' signs and wonders are more than a demonstration of his divinity. They are calculated to demonstrate that this Reign is already historical reality. There is One mightier at hand now, who conquers the might ones. Utopia is anticipated in moments of a topical liberation, for these moments point toward a perfect liberation of human beings and their cosmos. But an essential element of the reality of the Reign is the liquidation of death, for surely death is the direst enemy of human beings in their longing and striving for realization and fullness. It is for good reason that St. John substitutes the historical Jesus' own theme, that of the Reign of God, for "everlasting life."

But Jesus and his message have been rejected. Thus the realization of the Reign has been prevented. But a God who triumphs in human weakness and fragility has concretized his Reign nonetheless—in the reality of Jesus. In Jesus, utopia ("no place") becomes very *topos*, very much a place. "No place"? Nothing of the kind! The life manifested in Jesus as unrestricted gift, intimacy with God, love and fidelity to the death, has not been swallowed up in death. It has passed through the hell of our condition, yes, but then it has burst upon us with the force of a transfiguration we call Resurrection. St. Paul understood it well when he exclaimed, transported, "Death is swallowed up in victory. O death, where is your victory? O death, where is your sting" (1 Cor. 15:54–55).

Without the Resurrection, Christ would be an admirable human being, surely, a prophet who had chosen the most difficult path to tread in the defense of the cause of the oppressed, a martyr who sacrificed his life in the hope of something greater. But admirable is all that he would be. The cross would have meant the end of him. With the Resurrection, the truth about utopia has come to light: not death, but life is the last word pronounced by God on human destiny. Jesus is not only an object of admiration, he is an object of adoration.

Our future is open now. Now the historical course of life-and-death has a happy outcome, an end guaranteed and anticipated at the very heart of that historical trajectory. And behold, human consciousness suddenly knows a thing unknown to the whole ancient world: the smile of hope. The pagan world knew, to be sure, the belly laugh of a Pan or a Bacchus, the besotted, laughing din of a reeling Dionysus. Yes, and it has shown us the sad smile of one who lives under *Moirai* or *Fatum.* But it never knew the smile of One who has seen death and survived to tell the tale, enjoying the firstfruits of everlasting life. What is present reality for Jesus is the next thing in store for the rest of us. Well may we proclaim and believe in Jesus as the "last Adam" (1 Cor. 15:45), the new human being at long last emerging from the dregs of history.

LIFE CALLED TO LIFE

What is the relevance of the Resurrection for the human phenomenon? The Resurrection event responds to the basic conundrums of our existence. What is life? What is the future of life? This is the sort of vital question on which the Resurrection sheds an explanatory light. We need only glance around us to appreciate the iron grip of death. Life is all around us, yes, but so is death, because all ages, deteriorates, and finally dies.

Despite its mortality, however, life is a mystery. Science itself never tires of repeating this. We can study the conditions for life, but life itself is ever an open, challenging reality. True, wherever there is life there is an exchange of matter with a release of energy, and conservation of the species by way of multiplication. But all life knows a limit, even in those very low life forms that can maintain themselves in life for thousands upon thousands of years. Bacteria found in the hide of a mammoth more than ten thousand years old, found frozen in the wastelands of Siberia, were resuscitated. Mineral salts may contain bacteria in a state of suspended animation that can likewise be resuscitated, after thousands, even millions, of years. It is common nowadays to subject bacteria to extreme cooling to preserve them in a state in which they have no need for nutrition or reproduction: more than forty years later they can still be reactivated, and they will resume all of their vital functions.

And yet, even for the oldest of beings, the day comes when it, too, dies. For humanity, death has always meant trauma and anguish. Our whole being cries out for life in its fullness. Yet we are incapable of holding back the mechanisms of death. St. Paul voiced our desperation: "Who can free me from this body under the power of death?" But then he can say, "All praise to God, through Jesus Christ our Lord" (Rom. 7:24–25).

And in Paul's triumphant cry lies the Christian's interpretative key to the human drama. In Someone, life crying out for life has triumphed. In Someone, life maintains its force against the panting voracity of death. This is the meaning of the Resurrection for the human phenomenon. Resurrection does not say simply, We shall survive. The great philosophies have always taught as much. Resurrection says that the mortal life of humanity does not die for good, that life contains the possibility of a fulfillment so solid, so perfect, that death simply fails to penetrate it and perpetrate its deed of destruction. Our joy is in the certitude that this event of ultimate sweetness is not restricted to Christ alone. In the light of his Resurrection we discover that all life will inherit his Resurrection. The anguish of the ages vanishes, and our hearts are calm. Life is called to life. This is its Creator's design.

WE DIE TO BE RAISED

The New Testament occasionally presents other resurrections occurring before the final term of creation. Jesus' dialogue with Mary about the death of Lazarus explains why. Jesus promises Mary, "Your brother will rise again" (John 11:23). Mary, steeped in the culture of the Old Testament and its teaching of a Resurrection at the consummation of the ages, rightly replies, "I know he will rise again . . . in the resurrection on the last day" (John 11:24). But then Jesus makes the transition to the New Testament with the revelation of something new on the face of the Earth: "I am the resurrection and the life: whoever believes in me, though he should die, will come to life" (John 11:25–26).

Jesus draws the Resurrection event into our own history, a history still in course. Belief in Jesus, especially for the writers of the New Testament, is not a mere attachment to his Person and message. To believe in Jesus is to live the way he lived, to live our being as he lived his. If we live in gift, then—if we generate relationships of a communion of sisters and brothers, if we are able to rise above mechanisms of vengeance, if we open ourselves to the nameless Mystery Christians call God—then we find ourselves penetrated by the dynamisms of Resurrection. And in our death we unleash life, with all its might.

In the death of a human being of the quality of Jesus, a fragment of the world, a fragment of history, reaches its fullness. A renowned professor at the Pontifical Gregorian University in Rome, Juan Alfaro, citing the well-known Catholic theologian G. Greshake, says

A human being appears on the face of the universe not as a pure spirit, but in his or her concrete existence, sealed by whatever free decisions this human being may have made in the process of the transformation of the world. In a process of free action upon the world, in the course of a life of contact with this world and its ongoing history, this particular human being has concretely molded his or her own spirit to a determinate form and shape. Thus the death of this man or woman has a new meaning even for God: here is a new fragment of the world, a new fragment of history, finalized in this human being, in his or her death. And with each such death, God extends his dominion, gradually taking possession of the world and history for good and all.

Here is Resurrection in the very moment of death. Not that Resurrection is present only in death. Death is but the moment when Resurrection makes its appearance, when it irrupts. Resurrection has been here in this human life all along, present as a life process at the very heart of its mortality. Wherever, in mortal life, goodness triumphs over the instincts of hatred, wherever one heart opens to another, wherever a righteous attitude is built and room is created for God, there the Resurrection has begun. Death only pops open the pod: now the seeds fly in all directions, and life's meadow, smiling with flowers, explodes in beauty.

WHAT MUST A RISEN LIFE BE LIKE?

Just what would a raised, a resurrected life be like? In order to answer this question, we must contemplate the only resurrection event available for our consideration: the risen Christ. First, then, a risen life is a genuinely *human* life. It is the same individual—here, Jesus—who has died and who is now enthroned in the fullness of life. The one who has now been raised is none other than the one who walked among us doing good, the Crucified One. In the life of the Resurrection, the body as well as the soul is preserved and transfigured. We are not, then, dealing with a merely spiritual immortality, the immortality of one part only of the human being. The human being whole and entire is introduced into transfigured life.

Second, we must see the Resurrection as *new* life—not *another* life, to be sure, as the life here restored is numerically identical with the old one—but a new life nevertheless. After all, God has power to transform old to new, and the dead into the living. St. Paul is explicit: "This corruptible body must be clothed with incorruptibility, this mortal body with immortality" (1 Cor. 15:53). In a phrase, Resurrection introduces a transfiguration of mortal life.

Finally, a raised life is a *full* life. And what is a human being's fullness of life? We reach fullness of life when all of our latent dynamisms are expressed and activated. Now, the basic dynamism of life, even in the lower orders, is that of a mutual exchange, of giving and receiving, of communion. In the human being, to live signifies simply to commune—to enter into a relation with all beings, to elevate to its maximum potential the openness that this human being is presently realizing.

We can realize exalted forms of communion and sharing even in our present life. Through our bodies we make ourselves present to one another. Through thought and love we penetrate to the very intimacy of the other, and establish bonds of profound unity. But we always collide with immovable obstacles to communion. The body is surely the great vehicle of presence. Indeed, the body *is* presence. Yet it is also an obstacle to communion. It cannot be everywhere at once. We need space and time to move about and render ourselves present to other persons in other places. Or again, the body is not transparent. We generally communicate by words, signs, gestures—a universe of symbols inevitably fraught with ambiguity. The ideal would be—and this is our supreme aspiration—to rise above all of these impediments to communion and be totally transparent to one another. The utopia of the heart is a penetration of the intimacy of all things, a life of radical communion with the whole universe.

The Resurrection should be represented as the complete, exhaustive actualization of all the potentiality for communion residing within our human life. In Resurrection the human being comes to full flower. The buds of communion, of delicate openness to others, finally open. The fullness of life, the fullness of the Reign of the Father, is present at last.

"THE EXECUTIONER SHALL NOT TRIUMPH OVER THE VICTIM"

One question remains, a question arising out of our social existence. It torments our minds and spirits. The Resurrection of the Crucified One sheds a ray of light on it. The question is, What sense, what meaning, can there be in the violent deaths of those who have committed themselves to the cause of justice? What of the workers, the peasants, the Amerindians, the anonymous throng crucified in history, because they demanded their rights? History is usually written by the victors, and the victors write that history from the viewpoint of their victory. Who will pay for the suffering of the vanquished?

But the One who has been raised was one of these crushed and crucified ones—Jesus, the Suffering Servant. It was not a Caesar at the peak of his glory, or a general at the apogee of his armed might, or a sage at the height of his reputation who inherited the first-fruits of risen life. No, it was One committed to justice, especially to justice for the poor, and before he was raised his life was taken in a barbarous fashion. Surely those who have reached the top of the heap, who have a monopoly on power, possessions, or knowledge, may not define the final framework of a person's life, or the final, ultimate facts!

In Jesus' Resurrection God has shown that he sides with the crucified of history. The executioner shall not triumph over his victim. God has raised the victim, and thereby our thirst for a world of ultimate justice, a world of a communion of sisters and brothers at the last, is not cheated. "Insurrection" against injustice confers a new meaning on *Resurrection.* Those who "rise up" to do battle for justice will rise up to new life as well.

And so our thirst for life will not be left unslaked even if a collective holocaust awaits humanity. The destruction of the species, the annihilation of culture, the shriveling up and dying out of living nature, is not Earth's final destiny. Such a disaster will never prevent the realization of our true destiny as intended by God. The path would surely be a dramatic one, but the drama would not be a tragedy, any more than the personal life of Jesus of Nazareth issued in tragedy. The Book of Revelation, after describing the tribulations of the end, concludes with a victory hymn:

> Mighty and wonderful are your works,
> Lord God Almighty!
> Righteous and true are your ways,
> O King of the nations!
>
> Rev. 15:3

In view of the happy outcome, all roads leading to that outcome, however traumatic or tortured, will be seen in the end to have been good. Christians will, of course, struggle by all possible means to avoid the intrahistorical apocalypse threatening us today by reason of the excessive arrogance, the hubris, of the mighty. But it is not permitted to Christians to despair, as if this were all there were. The vision of the Christian is that of the Book of Revelation: "Then I saw new heavens and a new earth. The former heavens and the former earth had passed away" (Rev. 21:1). The disappearance of this old world makes room for a new one, then, one in which God will finally dwell with us and we shall be members of his family, his daughters and sons forever (Rev. 21:7).

In conclusion: In Jesus who was raised, Jesus the brother of our tortured human race, we discover the realization of the most radical utopia. The roots of this utopia are in the most archetypal dreams of our collective unconscious. But for those who can believe, none of this is utopia any longer, none of this is mere hope. No, all this is historical event, historical actuality, the legacy of all the just and the final destiny of the Earth that we defend and love in such fear and trembling.

Notes

CHAPTER 1. THEOLOGY OF LIBERATION: CREATIVE ACCEPTANCE OF VATICAN II FROM THE VIEWPOINT OF THE POOR

1. See the various studies on the aftermath of the Council, "Il Concilio tra continuità e involuzione," *Internazionale IDOC,* 1982, nos. 10, 11, 12.
2. Cf. Eric J. Hobsbawn, *Industry and Empire: From 1750 to the Present Day* (Harmondsworth, Pa.: Penguin, 1982); idem, *The Age of Revolution, Europe 1789–1848* (London: Sphere, 1984). For the basic questions, see Jean Ladrière, *Os desafios da racionalidade: O desafio da ciência e da técnica às culturas* (Petrópolis, Brazil: Vozes, 1980).
3. Cf. Pietro Scoppola, *Crisi modernista e rinnovamento cattolico in Italia* (Bologna: Mulino, 1969), 261–326; Emile Poulat, *Histoire, dogme et critique dans la crise moderniste* (Paris: Casterman, 1962); Jean Steinmann, *Friedrich von Hügel, sa vie, son oeuvre et ses amities* (Paris: Aubier, 1962), 389–454.
4. Cf. Joseph Ratzinger, "Kirche und Welt: zur Frage nach der Rezeption des II. Vatikanischen Konzils," in his *Theologische Prinzipienlehre: Bausteine zur Fundamentaltheologie* (Munich: Wewel, 1982), 397: "By 'world' it would seem we are to understand the totality of scientific and technological reality, along with the human beings who are the vessels of that reality and in whose mentality that reality is at home."
5. Verbatim citations of the documents of the Second Vatican Council are excerpted from Walter M. Abbott, ed., *The Documents of Vatican II* (New York: Herder and Herder Association, 1966).
6. Cf. Leonardo Boff, *A fé na periferia do mundo,* 3rd ed. (Petrópolis, Brazil: Vozes, 1983), 76–94.
7. Cf. José Comblin, "Secularization: Myths and Real Issues," trans. John Drury, *Concilium* 47 (1969):121–33, ed. Roger Aubert); various authors, *Les deux visages de la théologie de la sécularisation: analyse critique de la théologie de la sécularisation* (Paris and Tournai: Casterman, 1970).
8. For a good survey of the various tendencies of political theology, see Siegfried Wiedenhofer, *Politische Theologie* (Stuttgart: Kohlhammer, 1976).
9. Jürgen Moltmann, *Theology of Hope: On the Ground and the Implications of a Christian Eschatology* (New York: Harper & Row, 1975); idem, "Hacia una hermenéutica política del evangelio," *Cristianismo y Sociedad,* 24–25 (1970): 6–22.
10. Cf. Trutz Rendtorff and Heinz Eduard Tödt, *Theologie der Revolution: Analysen und Materialen* (Frankfurt am Main: Sührkamp, 1968); Hugo Assmann, "Caracterização de uma teologia da revolução," *Ponto Homem* 4 (1968):6–58; Otto Maduro, *Revelación y revolución: notas sobre el mensaje de los pueblos de América del imperialismo y de los capitalistas* (Merida, Venezuela: University de los Andes,

1970). For an ample bibliography on the subject, see Ernst Feil and Rudolf Weth, eds., *Diskussion zur "Theologie der Revolution"* (Munich and Mainz: Kaiser, 1969), 365–76.

11. Hugo Assmann, *Theology for a Nomad Church*, trans. Paul Burns (Maryknoll, N.Y.: Orbis, 1976), 88.

12. Cf. Johannes B. Metz, "Erlösung und Emanzipation," in Rudolph Affemann et al., *Erlösung und Emanzipation, Quaestiones Disputatae 61* (Freiburg: Herder, 1973), 120–40; Rubem A. Alves, *Tomorrow's Child: Imagination, Creativity, and the Rebirth of Culture* (New York: Harper & Row, 1972).

13. See the reflections of Gustavo Gutiérrez, *The Power of the Poor in History*, trans. Robert R. Barr (Maryknoll, N.Y.: Orbis, 1983), 167–234.

14. See the five volumes by Boaventura Kloppenburg, *Concilio Vaticano II* (Petrópolis, Brazil: 1962–65), still of value despite the reactionary attitudes espoused by the author beginning in the mid-1970s; for Dom Hélder Câmara, see the detailed report by M. Bandeira, "Dom Hélder Câmara e o Vaticano II," *Vozes* 72 (1978): 793–96.

15. See the fine summary by Hans Zwiefelhofer, "Zum Begriff der Dependenz," in Karl Rahner et al., *Befreiende Theologie: Der Beitrag Lateinamerikas zur Theologie der Gegenwart* (Stuttgart, Berlin, Cologne, and Mainz: Kohlhammer, 1977), 34–45.

16. A good introduction to this issue is O. Noggler, "Das erste Entwicklungsjahrzent: Vom II. Vatikanischen Konzil bis Medellín," in *Lateinamerika: Gesellschaft, Kirche, Theologie*, vol. 1, *Aufbruch und Auseinandersetzung*, ed. Hans-Jürgen Prien (Göttingen: Vandenhoeck und Ruprecht, 1981), 19–70.

17. For the history of this theology, see Roberto Oliveros Maqueo, *Liberación y teología: génesis y crecimiento de una reflexión 1966–77* (Lima: Centro de Estudios y Publicaciones, 1980); A. G. Rubio, *Teologia da libertação, política ou profetismo? Visão panorâmica e crítica da teologia política latino-americana* (São Paulo: Loyola, 1977); various authors, *História da teologia na América Latina* (São Paulo: Paulinas, 1981), esp. 139–64; José Comblin, "Kurze Geschichte der Theologie der Befreiung," in Prien, *Lateinamerika: Gesellschaft, Kirche, Theologie*, 1:13–38; Leonardo Boff, *O caminhar da Igreja com os oprimidos: do vale de lagrimas à terra prometida* (Rio de Janeiro: CODECRI, 1981), 181–95.

18. Cf. Clodovis Boff, "A dimensão teologal da política: da fé e daquilo que lhe pertenece," *Revista Eclesiástica Brasileira* 38 (1978):244–68; idem, *Comunidade eclesial—comunidade política: ensaios de eclesiologia política* (Petrópolis, Brazil: Vozes, 1978), esp. 64–84.

19. Cf. Segundo Galilea, *Teologia da libertação: ensaio de síntese* (São Paulo, 1978), 13–14); Juan Luis Segundo, *The Liberation of Theology*, trans. John Drury (Maryknoll, N.Y.: Orbis, 1976), 7–38.

20. For this theme, see the most satisfactory bibliography Yves M.-J. Congar, "La 'réception' comme réalité ecclésiologique," *Revue des Sciences Philosophiques et Théologiques* 56 (1972):369–403; idem, "Quod omnes tangit ab omnibus tractari et approbari debet," *Rev. Hist. Franc. et Etr.* 36 (1958):210–59; Alois Grillmeier, "Konzil und Rezeption: Bemerkungen zu einem Thema der ökumenischen Diskussion," *Theologie und Philosophie* 45 (1970):321–52; Heinrich Bacht, "Vom Lehramt der Kirche und in der Kirche," *Catholica* 25 (1971):144–67; Bernard Sesboué, "Autorité et Magistère et vie de foi ecclésiale," *Nouvelle Revue Théologique* 93 (1971):337–62, esp. 350–51.

21. Congar, " 'Réception,' " 370.

22. Cf. L. Stan, "Über die Rezeption der Beschlüsse der ökumenischen Synoden seitens der Kirche," *Theologica* 40 (1969):158–68, reprinted in *Konzile und die ökumenische Bewegung* (Geneva: 1968), 77–80; the entire issue of *The Ecumenical Review* 22 (1970); Piet Fransen, "L'autorité des Concils," in *Problèmes de l'autorité* (Paris, 1962), 59–100, esp. 83–84; H. Müller, "Rezeption und Konsens in der Kirche: eine Anfrage an die Kanonistik," *Österreichisches Archiv für Kirchenrecht* 27 (1976):3–21; Wacław Hryniewicz, "Die ekklesiale Rezeption in der Sicht der orthodoxen Theologie," *Theologie und Glaube* 65 (1975):250–66; Georg Denzler, "The Authority and the Reception of Conciliar Decisions in Christendom," *Concilium* 167 (7/1983):13–18; *The Ecumenical Council—Its Significance in the Constitution of the Church,* ed. Peter Huizing and Knut Walf; Joseph Ratzinger, "Kirche und Welt" (n. 4).

23. Eduardo Fernandez Regatillo, *Institutiones Iuris Canonici,* vol. 1 (Santander, Spain Sal Terrae, 1961), 35–36; Hans Dombois, *Das Recht der Gnade: ökumenisches Kirchenrecht* (Witten: Luther, 1961), 825–36; Luigi De Luca, "L'accettazione popolare della legge canonica nel pensiero di Graziano e dei suoi interpreti," *Studia Gratiana* 3 (1955):193–276.

24. Bacht, "Vom Lehramt" (n. 20), 161; Congar, " 'Réception' " (n. 20), 385, 399.

25. Paul VI, *Octogesima Adveniens,* no. 4.

26. Rafael Avila P., *Teología, evangelización y liberación* (Bogotá: Paulinas, 1973), 61–70; Clodovis Boff, *Teologia e prática: a teologia do político e suas mediaçoes* (Petrópolis, Brazil: Vozes, 1978), 245–55 (in English: *Theology and Practice: Episteinological Foundations* trans. Robert R. Barr [Maryknoll, N.Y.: Orbis, 1987]); Severino Croatto, "Befreiung und Freiheit: biblische Hermeneutik für die Theologie der Befreiung," in *Lateinamerika,* vol. 2, *Der Streit um die Theologie der Befreiung,* ed. Prien (n. 16), 40–59; for basic questions, see Paul Ricoeur, *Sciences humaines et conditionnements de la foi* (Paris, 1969), 147–56; Jean Ladrière, "La théologie et le langage de l'interprétation," *Revue Théologique de Louvain* 1 (1970):241–67; idem, *Language and Belief,* trans. Garrett Barden (Dublin: Gill and Macmillan, 1972).

27. See Ratzinger, "Kirche und Welt" (n. 6), 408–9: "Reception of the Council has not even begun. What has splintered the Church in the last decades has not been the Council, but the refusal to accept it."

28. Pablo Richard, *La Iglesia latino-americana entre el temor y la esperanza: apuntes teológicos para la decada de los anos 80* (San José, Costa Rica: Departamento Ecuménico de Investigaciones, 1981).

29. *Between Honesty and Hope: Documents from and about the Church in Latin America. Issued at Lima by the Peruvian Bishops' Commission for Social Action,* trans. John Drury, Maryknoll Documentation Series (Maryknoll, N.Y.: Maryknoll, 1970), 213.

30. Gustavo Gutiérrez, *A Theology of Liberation: History, Politics and Salvation,* trans. and ed. Caridad Inda and John Eagleson (Maryknoll, N.Y.: Orbis, 1973). Published originally in December 1971 as *Teología de la Liberación: perspectivas* (Lima: CEP, 1971).

31. Hugo Assmann, *Opresion-liberación: desafio a los cristianos* (Montevideo, Uruguay: Tierra Nueva, 1971).

32. Leonardo Boff, *Jesus Christ Liberator: A Critical Christology for Our Time,* trans. Patrick Hughes (Maryknoll, N.Y.: Orbis, 1978). Originally published as *Jesus Cristo Libertador: ensaio de Cristologia Crítica para o nosso Tempo* (Petrópolis, Brazil: Vozes, 1972).

33. Cf. the title of the book by renowned Archbishop José Maria Pires, *Do centro para a margem* ("From the Center to the Margin") (Petrópolis, Brazil: Vozes, 1980).

34. Cf. various authors, *Teología desde el cautiverio* (Mexico City: Iglesia Nueva 1976); Leonardo Boff, *Teología desde el cautiverio,* (Bogotá: Indo-American Press Service, 1975).

35. Cardinal Paulo Evaristo Arns, archbishop of São Paulo, has devoted himself to this cause, body and soul. See *Desaparecidos en la Argentina = Disappeared in Argentina* (São Paulo: Comité de Defensa de Derechos Humanos en el Cono Sur, 1982), preface in Spanish and English.

36. Cf. Leonardo Boff, *Ecclesiogenesis: The Base Communities Reinvent the Church,* trans. Robert R. Barr (Maryknoll, N.Y.: Orbis, 1986); Almir Ribeiro Guimarães, *Comunidades de base no Brasil* (Petrópolis, Brazil: Vozes, 1978), presenting a synthesis of the evolution of the base, or grass roots, church.

37. J. Simões Jorge, *Puebla, libertação do homem pobre* (São Paulo: Loyola, 1981); Gutiérrez, *Power of the Poor* (n. 13).

38. Verbatim citations of the Puebla Final Document are excerpted from John Eagleson and Philip Scharper, eds., *Puebla and Beyond: Documentation and Commentary* (Maryknoll, N.Y.: Orbis, 1979).

39. Leonardo and Clodovis Boff, *Theology and Liberation: In Search of a Balance between Faith and Politics,* trans. Robert R. Barr (Maryknoll, N.Y.: Orbis, 1984).

40. Enrique D. Dussel, "Hipoteses para uma Historia da Teologia na America Latina (1492–1980)," in *História da teologia* (n. 17), 165–96.

41. *Teología desde el Tercer Mundo: documentos finales de los cinco congresos internacionales de la Asociación Ecuménica de Teólogos del Tercer Mundo* (San José, Costa Rica: Departamento Ecuménico de Investigaciones, 1982); Sergio Torres and Virginia Fabella, eds., *The Emergent Gospel: Theology from the Underside of History: Papers from the Ecumenical Dialogue of Third World Theologians, Dar-es-Salaam, August 5–12, 1976* (Maryknoll, N.Y.: Orbis, 1978); Virginia Fabella, ed., *Asia's Struggle for Full Humanity: Towards a Relevant Theology: Papers from the Asian Theological Conference, January 7–20, 1979, Wennappuwa, Sri Lanka* (Maryknoll, N.Y.: Orbis, 1980); Virginia Fabella and Sergio Torres, eds., *Doing Theology in a Divided World: Papers from the Sixth International Conference of Third World Theologians, January 5–13, 1983, Geneva, Switzerland* (Maryknoll, N.Y.: Orbis, 1985); Kofi Appiah-Kubi and Sergio Torres, eds., *African Theology en Route* (Maryknoll, N.Y.: Orbis, 1979): a collection of papers from the Pan-African Conference of Third World Theologians held in Accra, Ghana.

42. For further details, see Leonardo Boff, "Die Anliegen der Befreiungstheologie," in *Wege theologischen Denkens,* Theologische Berichte, vol. 8 (Zurich, Einsiedeln, Cologne: Benziger, 1979), 70–103, esp. 78–79.

43. Leonardo Boff, *Teologia à escuta do povo* (Petrópolis, Brazil: Vozes, 1981), 113–18.

CHAPTER 2. MISSION OF THE CHURCH IN LATIN AMERICA: TO BE THE GOOD SAMARITAN

1. For the exegesis of this parable, see I. Howard Marshall, *The Gospel of Luke: A Commentary on the Greek Text* (Grand Rapids, Mich.: Eerdmans; Exeter: Paternoster, 1978), 444–50; Werner Monselewski, *Der barmherzige Samariter: eine aus-*

legungsgeschichtliche Untersuchung zu Lukas 10:25–37, Beiträge zur Geschichte der biblischen Exegese, vol. 5 (Tübingen: Mohr, 1967); G. Sellin, "Lukas als Gleichniserzähler: Die Erzählung vom barmherzigen Samariter," *Zeitschrift für Neutestamentliche Wissenschaft* 66 (1975):19–60; R. Eulenstein, "Und wer ist mein Nächster (Lk 10:25–37)?" *Theologie und Glaube* 67 (1977):127–45.

2. José Comblin et al., *La misión desde América Latina*, CLAR, vol. 11 (Bogotá: CLAR, 1982).

3. See the very instructive *Para entender América Latina: Aporte colectivo de los científicos sociales en Puebla*, Colleccion DEI, ed. Xabier Gorostiaga (Ciudad Universitaria Rodrigo Facio, Costa Rica: Editorial Universitaria Centro Americana, 1979).

4. Bartolomé de las Casas, *Brevísima relación de la destrucción de las Indias* (Buenos Aires: Editorial Universitaria de Buenos Aires, 1966), 36; in English: *Tears of the Indians: Being an Historical and True Account of the Cruel Massacres and Slaughters Committed by the Spaniards in the Islands of the West Indies, Mexico, Peru, etc.*, trans. (London, 1656) John Phillips (New York: Oriole, 1972); cf. E. Hoornaert, "Las Casas ou Sepúlveda?" *Revista Eclesiástica Brasileira* 30 (1970):850–70.

5. As cited by Enrique D. Dussel, *El episcopado latinoamericano y la liberación de los pobres, 1504–1620* (Mexico City: Centro de Reflexión Teológica, 1979), 89; cf. 89–95.

6. Cf. ibid., 18–19.

7. Verbatim citations of the Puebla Final Document are excerpted from John Eagleson and Philip Scharper, eds., *Puebla and Beyond: Documentation and Commentary* (Maryknoll, N.Y.: Orbis, 1979).

8. For this entire question, see Enrique D. Dussel, "Ensaio de síntese: hipóteses para uma história da teologia na América Latina (1492–1980)," in various authors, *História da teologia na América Latina* (São Paulo: Paulinas, 1981), 165–98.

9. See Ronaldo Muñoz, *Evangelio y liberación en América Latina: la teología pastoral de Puebla*, CLAR, no. 4 (Bogotá: Confederación Latinoamericana de Religiosos, Secretariado General; distributed by Indo-American Press Service 1980); idem, "O serviço da Igreja ao homem," *Revista Eclesiástica Brasileira* 35 (1975):824–35.

10. John Paul II, "Opening Address at the Puebla Conference," III, 4, in *Puebla and Beyond*, ed. John Eagleson and Philip Scharper, trans. John Drury (Maryknoll, N.Y.: Orbis, 1979), 67.

11. Verbatim citations of the documents of the Second Vatican Council are excerpted from Walter M. Abbott, ed., *The Documents of Vatican II* (New York: Herder and Herder; Association, 1966).

12. José Maria Pires, *Do centro para a margem* (Petropólis, Brazil: Vozes, 1980), 11–12, 127–33.

13. Cf. Jon Sobrino, *The True Church and the Poor*, trans. Matthew J. O'Connell (Maryknoll, N.Y.: Orbis, 1984), 160–93.

14. Cited by Gustavo Gutiérrez, *The Power of the Poor in History*, trans. Robert R. Barr (Maryknoll, N.Y.: Orbis, 1983), 195.

15. For this entire question, cf. Leonardo Boff, *O caminhar da Igreja com os oprimidos: do vale de lágrimas à terra prometida* (Rio de Janeiro: CODECRI, 1980); José Ignacio et al., *La justicia que brota de la fe (Rm 9,30)*, Coleccion Presencia Teologica (Santander Spain: Sal Terrae, 1982), esp. 201–202.

16. John Paul II, "Opening Address," III, 3, 66.

17. Cf. the presentation of the theology of liberation in Roberto Oliveros Maqueo, *Liberación y teología: génesis y crecimento de una reflexión 1966–77* (Lima: Centro de Estudios y Publicaciones, 1980); A. G. Rubio, *Teologia da libertação, política ou*

profetismo? Visão panorâmica e crítica da teologia política latino-americana (São Paulo: Loyola, 1977); Leonardo Boff, *Teologia do cativeiro e da libertação,* 3rd ed. (Petrópolis, Brazil: Vozes, 1983).

18. Cf. various authors, *Praxis del martirio, ayer y hoy* (Bogotá: Centro de Estudios y Publicaciones, 1977); Instituto Histórico Centro-Americano de Managua, *Sangue pelo povo (Martirológio latino-americano)* (Petrópolis, Brazil: Vozes, 1984).
19. Cf. Paulo Evaristo Cardinal Arns, *Os direitos humanos e a tareja da Igreja* (São Paulo: Loyola, 1976); Leonardo Boff, "Direitos dos pobres como direitos divinos," *SEDOC* 14 (1982), cols. 1033–41.
20. See *Revista Eclesiástica Brasileira* 34 (1974):934–6.
21. Cf. *Desaparecidos en la Argentina—Disappeared in Argentina* (São Paulo: Comité de Defensa de Derechos Humanos en el Cono Sur, 1982), preface in Spanish and English.
22. Cf. the documentation in *SEDOC* 14 (1982), the entire May issue, and 15 (1983), the entire June issue.
23. The principal texts were compiled in *Una Iglesia que nace del pueblo* (Salamanca, Spain: Sígueme, 1979). Cf. various authors, *Cruz y resurrección: Presencia y anuncio de una Iglesia nueva* (Mexico City, 1978); José Galea, *Uma Igreja no povo e pelo povo: Reflexão teológica sobre a atual ação pastoral da Igreja no Brasil* (Petrópolis, Brazil: Vozes, 1983); Ronaldo Muñoz, *La Iglesia en el pueblo: Hacia una eclesiología latinoamericana* (Lima: Centro de Estudios y Publicaciones, 1983); Leonardo Boff, *Ecclesiogenesis: The Base Communities Reinvent the Church,* trans. Robert R. Barr (Maryknoll, N.Y.: Orbis, 1986); idem, *Church, Charism and Power: Liberation Theology and the Institutional Church,* trans. John W. Diercksmeier (New York: Crossroad, 1985).
24. See the text in *SEDOC* 15 (1982), cols. 498–502.
25. *Revista Eclesiástica Brasileira* 41 (1981):834–35.

CHAPTER 3. RIGHTS OF THE POOR: RIGHTS OF GOD

1. See Hubert Lepargneur, "A Igreja e o reconhecimento dos diretos humanos," part 1, *Revista Eclesiástica Brasileira* 37 (1977):178; see also more detailed studies, such as that of Philippe de la Chapelle, *La déclaration universelle des droits de l'homme et de catholicisme* (Paris: Librairie générale de droit et de jurisprudence, 1967); *Concilium* 124 (4/1979), ed. Alois Müller and Norbert Greinacher; M. Schooyans, *Droits de l'homme et technocratie* (Chambray, 1982), 14–19, 23–52; Paul Hinder, *Grundrechte in der Kirche: Zur Begründung der Grundrechte in der Kirche* (Freiburg: Universitätsverlag, 1977), 11–38.
2. Hubert Lepargneur, "Igreja e reconhecimento," part 2, 181, n. 51.
3. Enrique D. Dussel, "Modern Christianity in Face of the 'Other' (From the 'Rude' Indian to the 'Noble Savage')," *Concilium* 130 (10/1979):49–59, ed. Jacques Pohier and Dietmar Mieth.
4. Ibid.
5. Enrique D. Dussel, *El episcopado latinoamericano y la liberacion de los pobres 1504–1620* (Mexico City: Centro de Reflexión Teológica, 1979), 19.
6. In *Revista Eclesiástica Brasileira* 34 (1974):934–36.
7. Jon Sobrino, "Dios y los procesos revolucionarios," in *Apuntes para una Teología Nicaragüense* (San José, Costa Rica: Departamento Ecumenico de Investigaciones, 1980), the entire third part.
8. *Revista Eclesiástica Brasileira* 34 (1974):935.

9. Verbatim citations of the Puebla Final Document are excerpted from John Eagleson and Philip Scharper, eds., *Puebla and Beyond: Documentation and Commentary* (Maryknoll, N.Y.: Orbis, 1979).

CHAPTER 4. THE SUPERNATURAL IN THE PROCESS OF LIBERATION

1. Cf. G. Colombo, "Sopranaturale: Il tramonto del termine 'sopranaturale,' " in *Dizionario Teologico Interdisciplinare*, vol. 3 (Turin: Marietti, 1977), 297–301.
2. See Leonardo Boff, *A graça libertadora no mundo* (Petrópolis, Brazil: Vozes, 1977), 56–62)—English translation, *Liberating Grace*, trans. John Drury (Maryknoll, N.Y.: Orbis, 1979); Juan Alfaro, *Cristología y antropología: temas teológicos actuales* (Madrid: Cristiandad, 1973), 227–343, 345–66.
3. For a study of the word, see Henri de Lubac's classic *Le Surnaturel* (Paris: Aubier, 1946), 325–94.
4. Cf. ibid., 369.
5. For this entire question, see the erudite study of G. Colombo, "Il problema del sopranaturale negli ultimi cinquant' anni," in *Problemi e orientamenti di teologia dommatica*, vol. 2 (Milan, 1957), 547–607; idem, "Grazia," in *Enciclopedia delle Religioni*, vol. 1 (Florence: Vallecchi, 1970), 1612–46; B. Gherardini, "Naturale e sopranaturale: una precisazione," *Divinitas* 19 (1975):139–58; Gianpiero Bof, "Sobrenatural," in *Nuevo Diccionario de Teología*, ed. G. Barbaglio and S. Dianich, vol. 2 (Madrid: Cristiandad, 1982), 1673–87.
6. Cf. A. Vanneste, "Le mystère du surnaturel," *Ephemerides Theologicae Lovanienses* 44 (1968):179–90.
7. Cf. Maurizio Flick and Zoltán Alszeghy, *Fondamenti di una antropologia teologica* (Florence: Libreria Editrice Fiorentina, 1970), 433.
8. See Pablo Richard, *A Igreja latino-americana entre o temor e a esperança* (São Paulo: Loyola, 1982), 13–34: esp. 25–30. Spanish original: *La iglesia latino-americana entre el temor y la esperanza: apuntes teológicos para la decada de los años 80* (San José, Costa Rica: Departamento Ecuménico de Investigaciones).
9. On the theology of liberation, see these historico-synthetic studies: A. G. Rubio, *Teologia da libertaçao, política ou profetismo? Visão panorâmica e crítica da teologia política latino-americana* (São Paulo: Loyola, 1977); Roberto Oliveros Maqueo, *Liberación y teología: génesis y crecimiento de una reflexión 1966–77* (Lima: Centro de Estudios y Publicaciones, 1980); Leonardo and Clodovis Boff, *Salvation and Liberation: In Search of a Balance between Faith and Politics,* trans. Robert R. Barr (Maryknoll, N.Y.: Orbis, 1984).
10. See my study in homage to Karl Rahner on the occasion of his eightieth birthday, appearing as Chapter 1 of the present volume.
11. Cf. Gustavo Gutiérrez, *A Theology of Liberation* (Maryknoll, N.Y.: Orbis, 1973), 69–72.
12. Verbatim citations of the Puebla Final Document are excerpted from John Eagleson and Philip Scharper, eds., *Puebla and Beyond: Documentation and Commentary* (Maryknoll, N.Y.: Orbis, 1979).
13. See the best study on the subject: Clodovis Boff, *Teologia e prática: A teologia do político e suas mediações* (Petrópolis, Brazil: Vozes, 1978). In English: *Theology and Praxis*, trans. Robert R. Barr (Maryknoll, N.Y.: Orbis, 1987).

14. The verbatim citations of *Evangelii Nuntiandi* here and throughout this chapter are excerpted from *On Evangelization in the Modern World: Pope Paul VI* (Washington, D.C.: United States Catholic Conference, 1976).

15. For the various models of the relationship between the salvation of Jesus Christ and historical liberation, see Leonardo and Clodovis Boff, *Salvation and Liberation* (n. 9), 56–64.

16. Cf. *SEDOC* 11 (1978), cols. 386–88, 392–93.

CHAPTER 5. HOW OUGHT WE TO CELEBRATE THE EUCHARIST IN A WORLD OF INJUSTICE?

1. A minimal bibliography must include J. Betz, "Eucaristia: misterio central," in Johannes Feiner and Magnus Lohrer, eds., *Mysterium Salutis*, vol. 4/5 (Petrópolis, Brazil: Vozes, 1977)—German original: 4th ed. (Einsiedeln: Benziger, 1978); F.-X. Durrwell, *L'Eucharistie, sacrement pascal* (Paris: Cerf, 1981); various authors, *L'Eucharistie: de Jésus aux chrétiens d'aujourd'hui* (Limoges: Droguet et Ardant, 1981); for a sense of the orientation of recent research, see Raymond Winling, *La théologie contemporaine (1945–1980)* (Paris: Centurion, 1983), 420–29.

2. For the exegetical background, see Alexander Gerken, *Theologie der Eucharistie* (Munich: Kösel, 1973), 17–60.

3. For this entire question, see Leonardo Boff, *Paixão de Cristo—Paixão do mundo* (Petrópolis, Brazil: Vozes, 1978), 25–59. English translation: *Passion of Christ, Passion of the World*, trans. Robert R. Barr (Maryknoll, N.Y.: Orbis, 1987).

4. Cf. Hugo Echegaray, *A prática de Jesus* (Petrópolis, Brazil: Vozes, 1982), 133–44. English translation: *The Practice of Jesus*, trans. Matthew J. O'Connell (Maryknoll, N.Y.: Orbis, 1984).

5. Irenaeus *Adversus Haereses* 4, 18, 2.

6. The most complete study is surely that of Antonio Piolanti, *The Holy Eucharist*, trans. Luigi Penzo (New York: Desclée, 1961).

7. For a survey of current theories, see Joseph Powers, *Eucharistic Theology* (New York: Herder, 1967), esp. 111–79; Otto Semmelroth, *Eucharistische Wandlung: Transsubstantion-Transfinalisation-Transsignifikation* (Kevelaer: Butzon & Bercker, 1967).

8. A sampling of the possible references here: José M. Castillo, *La alternativa cristiana: Hacia una iglesia del pueblo* (Salamanca: Sígueme, 1979), 302–21, 322–46; F. Barbero, "Verso la riscoperta e la riappropriazione dell'Eucaristia," in various authors, *Massa e Meriba: Itinerari di fede nella storia delle comunità di base* (Turin: Claudiana; Tempi di Fraternità, 1980), 306–28; André Manaranche, "Communion eucharistique et vie politique," *Cahiers de l'Actualité Religieuse et Sociale* 14 (1971):247–48; Gustavo Gutiérrez, *A Theology of Liberation* (Maryknoll, N.Y.: Orbis, 1973), 265–70; J.-P. Jossua and J. Mansir, *Divisions des chrétiens et vérité de l'Eucharistie* (Paris, 1972), 35–74; (J. Robert, "Peut-on eucharistiquement servir le Seigneur et l'argent?" *La Lettre* (1968), 1–6;) A. Rich, "La fonction politique du culte," *Revue de Théologie et de Philosophie* 8 (1971):65–79; (P. Jacquemont, "Du bon usage de l'eucharistie," *Informations Catholiques internationales* (1968), 6–7;) W. Elert, *Abendmahl und Kirchengemeinschaft in der alten Kirche, hauptsächlich des Ostens* (Berlin: Lutherisches Verlaghaus, 1954); Adalbert Hamman, *Vie liturgique et vie sociale: Repas des pauvres* (Paris, Rome, and New York: Desclée, 1968), with a most

rich bibliography on the practice of the early Church; B. de Clercq, "Engajamento político e celebração litúrgica," *Concilium* (Lisbon) (1973/4):482–88; *Concilium* 152 (1982), ed. Mary Collins and David Power, the entire issue; Segundo Galilea, "Les messes de protestation," *Parole et Mission* 14 (1971):334–35; Peter Cornehl and Hans-Eckehard Bahr, eds., *Gottesdienst und Öffentlichkeit* (Hamburg: Furche, 1970).

9. Richard Hentschke, *Die Stellung der vorexilischen Schriftpropheten zum Kultus* (Berlin: Töpelmann, 1957); Roland de Vaux, *Ancient Israel: Its Life and Institutions,* trans. John McHugh (New York: McGraw-Hill, 1951), 454–55.

10. Cf. H. W. Wolff, *Die Stunde des Amos: Prophetie und Protest* (Munich: Kaiser, 1969), 54–67.

11. J. M. Gonzalez Ruiz, *Concilium* 192 (1973/4).

12. The translation of this passage is in dispute among exegetes. I follow W. Rees, *A Catholic Commentary on the Holy Scripture* (London: 1952), 1093; José M. Castillo, 333–34; Elisabeth Schüssler Fiorenza, in *Concilium* 152 (1982), especially *sub fine.*

13. Cf. F.-X. Durrwell, *L'Eucharistie, sacrement pascal* (n. 1), 55.

14. See the shattering observations of Enrique D. Dussel, *Concilium* (Lisbon) (1982/2):76–88.

15. As cited by Gustavo Gutiérrez, *A Theology of Liberation* (n. 8), 264.

16. Pliny the Younger *Epistolae* 10, 96; see José M. Castillo, *La alternativa cristiana* (n. 8), "La eucaristia, problema político" 339.

17. *Didachē* 14, 2.

18. For a historical résumé of the issue, see José Ramos-Regidor, *El sacramento de la Penitencia* (Salamanca, Spain: Sígueme, 1975), 171–204.

19. Justin Martyr *Apology* 1, 67, 6.

20. Cyprian of Carthage *De Opere et Eleemosynis* 15; see Maria Grazia Mara, ed., *Ricchezza e povertà nel cristianesimo primitiva* (Rome: Città Nuova, 1980), 147–48.

21. *Didascalia Apostolorum* 4, 8, 2.

22. José M. Castillo, *La alternativa cristiana* (n. 8), 345.

CHAPTER 6. HOW OUGHT WE TO PREACH THE CROSS IN A CRUCIFIED SOCIETY TODAY?

1. See Leonardo Boff, *Paixão de Cristo—Paixão do mundo* (Petrópolis, Brazil: Vozes, 1978)—English translation, *Passion of Christ, Passion of the World,* trans. Robert R. Barr (Maryknoll, N.Y.: Orbis, 1987). I shall list several more Latin American titles, as it has been on this continent that the subject has received, in recent years, its most adequate development, especially in terms of its connections with the painful journey of the Church. Jon Sobrino, *Christology at the Crossroads,* trans. John Drury (Maryknoll, N.Y.: Orbis, 1978), 179–235; idem, *Jesús en América Latina* (Santander, Spain: Sal Terrae 1982), 235–50, 251–61—English translation, trans. Robert R. Barr (Maryknoll, N.Y.: Orbis, 1989); Ignacio Ellacuría, *Freedom Made Flesh: The Mission of Christ and His Church,* trans. John Drury (Maryknoll, N.Y.: Orbis, 1976), 21–79; idem, "El pueblo crucificado," in various authors, *Cruz y resurreccion* (Mexico City: Centro de Reflexión Teológica, 1978), 49–82; idem, "Pour qué muere Jesús y por qué le matan," *Misión Abierta* 2 (1977):17–26; Raul Vidales, "La prática histórica de Jesús:

Notas provisorias," *Christus* (Mexico City) 480 (1975): 43–55; Hugo Eche-garay, *A prática de Jesus* (Petrópolis, Brazil: Vozes, 1982), 111–52—in English, *The Practice of Jesus*, trans. Matthew J. O'Connell (Maryknoll, N.Y.: Orbis, 1984); Benedito Ferraro, *A significação política da morte de Jesus à luz do Novo Testamento* (Petrópolis, Brazil: Vozes, 1979)—also in *Revista Eclesiástica Brasileira* 36 (1976):811–57; José Ramos-Regidor, *Gesù e il risveglio degli oppressi: La sfida della teologia della liberazione* (Milan: Mondadori, 1981), esp. 269–353; José Miguez-Bonino, ed., *Faces of Jesus: Latin American Christologies*, trans. Robert R. Barr (Maryknoll, N.Y.: Orbis, 1984); along the same lines, see the important work of José Ignacio González Faus, *La humanidad nueva: Ensayo de cristología* (Barcelona and Madrid: Eapsa, 1974), 1:123–79, 2:519–65.

2. José Ignacio González Faus, *La humanidad nueva*, 1:144.

3. "To live is to die . . . to live better, to live more integrally, to live in immortal fashion" (Alceu Amoroso Lima, *Tudo é mistério* [Petrópolis, Brazil: Vozes, 1983], 82).

4. For more detail, see Leonardo Boff, *Paixão de Cristo* (n. 1), 67–68, 83–84, as well as *Grande Sinal* 36 (1982):360–65.

5. The mystics testify to this dimension. In 1897, shortly before her death, Saint Thérèse of the Child Jesus wrote, "It is not a veil for me, it is a wall, reaching to heaven and covering the starry firmament. When I sing the happiness of heaven, God's everlasting possession, I feel no joy, for I sing only what I wish to believe." On another occasion she wrote, "Move on, rejoice in death, which will give you not what you hope, but a night deeper still, a night of nothing. . . . I will write no more, for fear of blaspheming." A convert said, "Earlier, when I was an atheist, I felt an empty absence. Now I feel a full absence." Expressions such as these afford us a glimpse of the interior cross, which is every bit as painful as the physical one. For these and other examples, see Hubert Lepargneur, "Experience de Deus," *Grande Sinal* 36 (1982):278–82.

6. As cited by Enrique D. Dussel, *El episcopado latinoamericano y la liberación de los pobres 1504–1620* (Mexico City: Centro de Reflexión Teológica, 1979), 19, n. 18.

7. Pope John Paul II's very words in his inaugural discourse to the bishops of Puebla (part 3, no. 3). See John Eagleson and Philip Scharper, eds., *Puebla and Beyond: Documentation and Commentary* (Maryknoll, N.Y.: Orbis, 1979), 66.

8. As Ignacio Ellacuría correctly observes in his "El pueblo crucificado" (n. 1), 56:

An ascetical, moralizing focus on the Christian cross has stripped that cross of all historical importance, and encouraged people to reject anything connected with it. This rejection is fully justified, unless we have succeeded in wresting free of the emotional specters that haunt this symbol. The renewal of the mystery of the cross has absolutely nothing to do with repression for its own sake—which sets the cross where each of us would have it, instead of where it was placed by Jesus himself. Jesus' purpose was not death for its own sake, but the proclamation of the Kingdom.

9. See no. 1159 of the Puebla Final Document, in John Eagleson and Philip Scharper, *Puebla and Beyond* (n. 7), 267.

10. Ibid., nos. 79, 83 (pp. 133, 134).
11. See the entire *Concilium* 163 (3/1983), ed. Johannes-Baptist Metz and Edward Schillebeeckx, including material on martyrdom in its Latin American context.
12. Gustav Janouch, *Conversations with Kafka,* trans. Goronwy Rees (New York: New Directions, 1971), 134.
13. See the important book by Carlos Mesters, *O destino do povo que sofre* (Petrópolis, Brazil: Vozes, 1981).
14. See Jürgen Moltmann, *The Crucified God: The Cross of Christ and the Foundation and Criticism of Christian Theology* (New York: Harper & Row, 1974). Idem, "Prospettive dell'odierna teologia della croce," in *Sulla teologia della croce* (Brescia, 1972), 23–54, esp. 39–40.